T0113965

GOD
BLESS
THE
CRIMSON
TIDE

ED McMINN

Devotions for
the Die-Hard
Alabama Fan

GOD
BLESS
THE
CRIMSON
TIDE

HOWARD BOOKS
A DIVISION OF SIMON & SCHUSTER
New York   London   Toronto   Sydney

Our purpose at Howard Books is to:
• *Increase faith* in the hearts of growing Christians
• *Inspire holiness* in the lives of believers
• *Instill hope* in the hearts of struggling people everywhere
Because He's coming again!

Howard Books, a division of Simon & Schuster, Inc.
HOWARD 1230 Avenue of the Americas, New York, NY 10020
BOOKS
www.howardpublishing.com

God Bless the Crimson Tide © 2007 Ed McMinn

All rights reserved, including the right to reproduce this book or portions thereof
in any form whatsoever. For information, address Permission Department, Simon
& Schuster, 1230 Avenue of the Americas, New York, NY 10020.

Agent: Les Stobbe

Library of Congress Cataloging-in-Publication Data

13 Digit ISBN: 978-1-4165-4188-2
10 Digit ISBN: 1-4165-4188-8

13 Digit ISBN: 978-1-58229-639-5 (gift edition)
10 Digit ISBN: 1-58229-639-1 (gift edition)

10   9   8   7   6   5   4   3   2   1

HOWARD colophon is a registered trademark of Simon & Schuster, Inc.

Manufactured in the United States of America

For information regarding special discounts for bulk purchases,
please contact Simon & Schuster Special Sales at 1-800-456-6798
or business@simonandschuster.com.

Edited by Between the Lines
Cover design by John Lucas
Interior design by Jaime Putorti

Scripture quotations are taken from the New Revised Standard Version Bible.
Copyright © 1989 by the Division of Christian Education of the National Council
of the Churches of Christ in the United States of America. All rights reserved.

To Slynn and to David
I am your biggest fan

CONTENTS

GOD BLESS THE CRIMSON TIDE

The Outer Limits

Read Genesis 18:1–15.

"Is anything too wonderful for the LORD?" (v. 14).

A death set in motion the chain of events that made a young man bound for Yale the father of Alabama football.

According to Clyde Bolton in *The Crimson Tide,* in the late 1880s W. G. Little was prepping at Phillips-Exeter Academy in Andover, Massachusetts, on his way to Yale. But when his oldest brother, James, died, Little returned home to Livingston, Alabama, to be with his mother. He then enrolled at the local university, from which James had graduated. While he was at Phillips-Exeter, Little had been introduced to a new game called football. When he came to Alabama, Bolton said, Little "brought his canvas football suit, his cleated shoes, and his pigskin ball with him." This unusual baggage drew a lot of interest from his classmates, who responded with great enthusiasm when Little suggested they form a team.

A roster was assembled, the University Athletic Association was born, and a coach, Eugene Beaumont, was hired. Not surprisingly, Little was named the first football captain. On November 11, 1892, the University of Alabama played its first-ever football game. Their opponent was a team from Birmingham High School. Fittingly, considering Alabama's great history, the game was a rout. Alabama won 56–0.

The game W. G. Little had encountered in the Northeast had come south.

You've probably never tried a whole bunch of things you've dreamed about doing at one time or another. Like starting your own business. Going back to school. Running for elected office. Running a marathon. What holds you back? Perhaps you see only your limitations, both those you've imposed on yourself and those others have convinced you exist. But at the University of Alabama one student started the football program.

God sees your possibilities, not your limitations. Free yourself from that which ties your hands and blights your dreams by depending not on yourself but on God.

First, I prepare. Then I have faith.
—Joe Namath

➤ **God has a vision for your life beyond your imagining, but you have to depend on him, not on yourself.**

DAY 2

How We Leave

Read 2 Kings 2:1–12.

"A chariot of fire and horses of fire separated the two of them, and Elijah ascended in a whirlwind into heaven" (v. 11).

We can't always choose how we leave.

Even the coach who led Alabama to its first glory on the gridiron didn't go out the way he wanted to. In *Third Saturday in October* Al Browning called Wallace Wade the "Godfather" of Alabama football. Wade coached Alabama from 1923 to 1930; his record was 61–13–3. Under his leadership the Tide won the most significant game in the history of southern football to that time when they whipped Washington 20–19 in the 1926 Rose Bowl, establishing Alabama's program as a national power and earning respect for football in the region. Bear Bryant told Browning, "I tip my hat to Wallace Wade."

"Incredible as it seems," Browning said, "Wade was forced to move from Alabama by a proud school president, Dr. George Denny, who was apparently jealous of the strong hold the coach had over the Crimson Tide faithful."

John Henry Suther, an all-American halfback who played for Wade, told Browning, "Coach Wade and Dr. Denny never did see eye-to-eye. . . . Dr. Denny was always nosing around the practice field. . . . Coach Wade would tell him to get his fanny off the field so we could get some work done."

Wade admitted that he left Alabama bitter, though he told Browning in 1981, "I have since mellowed."

You probably haven't always chosen the moves you've made in your life. Perhaps your company transferred you. A landlord didn't renew your lease. An elderly parent needed your care.

Sometimes the only choice we have about leaving is whether we do so with style and grace. Our exit from life is the same way. Unless we usurp God's authority over life and death, we can't choose how we die, just how we handle it.

We do, however, control our destination. How we leave isn't up to us; where we spend eternity is—and that depends on our relationship with Jesus.

If I drop dead tomorrow, at least I know
I died in good health.

—PRO FOOTBALL COACH BUM PHILLIPS AFTER A PHYSICAL

> **When you go isn't up to you; where you go is.**

A Crowd of Witnesses

Read Hebrews 11:39–12:2.

"Since we are surrounded by so great a cloud of witnesses, . . . let us run with perseverance the race that is set before us" (v. 1).

According to "Alabama Gymnastics," the program wasn't much to speak of in 1978 when Sarah Campbell, just twenty-two years old, took the head coaching job without knowing what her salary would be or what facilities and equipment she'd have to work with. Maybe she should have asked.

The program was only four years old, had had four different coaches, and had not had a winning season. Serious talk was afloat about discontinuing the sport. Campbell and David Patterson, the man she hired as her assistant coach and eventually would marry, scoured the dormitories for students with any gymnastics experience just to fill out the squad.

The gymnasts shared their practice space with the volleyball team and frequently dodged stray volleyballs that zinged into the area. Patterson had to explain to an athletic director named Bryant why a wrestling mat with a hole in it wouldn't work as a floor exercise mat.

Interest in the program was reflected in attendance at meets. Only about three dozen people showed up to watch the team, and most of them were relatives of a team member. Those were lonely days for the Alabama gymnasts and their coaches.

Everyone spends time alone in life. A child's illness, the slow death of a loved one, financial troubles in business or at home, a question about your health—they all can bring feelings of isolation.

But a person of faith is never alone, and not just because you're aware of God's presence. You are always surrounded by a crowd of God's most faithful witnesses, those in the present and those from the past. With their examples before you, you can endure your trials, looking in hope and faithfulness beyond the immediate troubles to God's glorious future.

Remember those empty seats in the early days of the gymnastics program? Nowadays the squad draws more than nine thousand fans to a meet, a true "crowd of witnesses."

In life, you'll have your back up against the wall many times. You might as well get used to it.
—BEAR BRYANT

▷ **The example of the faithful who persevered despite trepidation and suffering calls you to be true to God no matter what besets you.**

DAY 4

Taking Action

Read James 2:14–26.

"Faith by itself, if it has no works, is dead" (v. 17).

Jeremiah Castille admitted he "probably said four words my whole four years" at Alabama. But on December 29, 1982, the all-American cornerback, who today has his own ministry, did something totally out of character: he stood up and made a speech.

What made this night so special that the quietest player of them all would feel the Lord call him to fire up his team? The occasion was the 1982 Liberty Bowl, the last game Bear Bryant would coach.

In *Legends of Alabama Football,* Richard Scott quoted Castille: "We were sitting there getting ready before the game, and the Lord just prompted me to let Coach Bryant know how much he had done for me, how much he meant to me." So Castille told the team, "I came here an eighteen-year-old boy and I'm leaving as a twenty-two-year-old man, and he had a lot to do with that. This is my last game, this is Coach Bryant's last game, and we're going out a winner. There's no way we're going to lose this."

The Tide defeated Illinois 21–15, thanks in part to three Castille interceptions.

Castille's unexpected and simple but poignant words certainly served as inspiration, but they would have been useless without subsequent action; not a single word he said intercepted a pass.

Talk is cheap. Consider your neighbor or coworker who talks without saying anything, who makes promises she doesn't keep, who brags about his own exploits, who can always tell you how to do something but never shows up for the work.

How often have you fidgeted through a meeting, impatient to get on with the work everybody is talking about doing? You know that speech without action just doesn't cut it.

The same is true for the person of faith: action shouts of true, living faith. Jesus Christ is alive; your faith should be, too.

> *Don't talk too much or too soon.*
> —BEAR BRYANT

➤ **Faith that does not reveal itself in action is dead.**

Toughing It Out

Read 2 Corinthians 11:21–29.

"Besides other things, I am under daily pressure because of my anxiety for all the churches" (v. 28).

Tackle W. T. "Bully" VandeGraaff, Alabama's first all-American, may have been the toughest Crimson Tide player ever. A Tennessee player—of all people—gushed to Al Browning in *Third Saturday in October* about how tough VandeGraaff was.

S. D. "Bull" Bayer was a Tennessee Volunteers tackle who played opposite Bully in the 1913 game, which Alabama won 6–0, its seventh straight shutout of the Volunteers. Bayer recalled that Bully had a cut at the top of one ear. "It was dangling from his head a bit, bleeding a lot," Bayer said. "He got his ear caught on the leg of my pants a play or two later, and he got so mad about it that he jumped to his feet, grabbed his ear and tried to yank it from his head."

Fortunately for Bully's appearance, his teammates stopped him and got him to the manager, who bandaged his ear so Bully could keep playing.

Such flinty resolve made an indelible impression on Bayer.

He told Browning, "Boy, was he a tough something. He wanted to throw away his ear so he could keep playing. In all my days in football, I never saw anything like that again."

VandeGraaff was one tough cookie, even for a Crimson Tide football player. But you don't have to rip off an ear to be tough. Going to work every morning, sticking to your rules for the children, always telling the truth, making hard decisions about your life—you've got to be strong every day just to live honorably, decently, and justly.

Living faithfully requires toughness, too, though in America you probably won't be imprisoned, stoned, or flogged for your faith, as the apostle Paul was. Still, society and popular culture exert subtle, psychological, daily pressures on you to turn your back on your faith and your values.

Hang tough: Keep the faith.

Winning isn't imperative,
but getting tougher in the fourth quarter is.
—BEAR BRYANT

> **Life demands more than mere physical toughness; you must be spiritually tough, too.**

Star Power

Read Luke 10:1–3, 17–20.

"The Lord appointed seventy others and sent them on ahead of him in pairs to every town and place where he himself intended to go" (v. 1).

Erin Heffner was a volleyball star, one of the greatest players in SEC history.

She left Alabama after the 2004 season as the school's career leader in both kills and total attacks, third in career digs, and fourth in career service aces. She led the SEC in kills per game as a junior and a senior. She was twice named all-SEC, all-district, and honorable mention all-American. She was the District Freshman of the Year in 2001 and eight times was named to an all-tournament team, the school record.

During her four years at Alabama, the volleyball record was 80–46, twenty wins a season. Heffner was the backbone of the Crimson Tide team—and then she was gone.

So what did the 2005 Alabama volleyball players do without her? They rolled to a 23–11 record, the second-highest win total since the program was revived in 1989, and received the school's first-ever bid to the NCAA Tournament.

Jessie Patterson wrote in his *Crimson White* article "Striking a Balance" that the "mantra" for the team was "balance." Sophomore Bridget Fuentez emerged as the team's go-to player, but she admitted success was a team effort. "It's great to be a part of the team and feel like you're helping your team out," she told Patterson. "It's not a one-person team this year."

The team known as a church isn't a one-person undertaking either, though it may have its "star" in the preacher. Preachers certainly are the most visible representative of a church team. After all, they are God's paid, trained professionals.

But when Jesus assembled seventy folks to work for him, he didn't have anybody on the payroll or any hotshots. All he had were no-names who loved him. And nothing has changed. God's church still depends on those whose only pay is the satisfaction of serving and whose only qualification is their love for God. God's church needs you.

You may have the greatest bunch of individual stars in the world, but if they don't play together, the club won't be worth a dime.
—BABE RUTH

 Yes, the church needs its professional clergy, but it also needs those who serve as volunteers because they love God; the church needs you.

A Second Chance

Read John 7:53–8:11.

"Jesus said, 'Neither do I condemn you. Go your way, and from now on do not sin again'" (v. 8:11).

Chad Goss needed a second chance.

In the biggest game of his life, the 1997 Outback Bowl against Michigan, he made the biggest mistake of his football career. With Alabama leading 17–6 and time running out, Goss stood alone at his ten-yard line to field the Wolverine punt that would clinch the win.

He told Wayne Atcheson in *Faith of the Crimson Tide*: "I thought I had only taken one step back. Instead, I had taken about eight steps back, and I fair caught the ball on the ONE YARD LINE." Coach Gene Stallings was waiting for him on the sidelines, and he wasn't smiling.

Goss's gloom deepened when Michigan held, took the Bama punt, and scored. With less than a minute left, Alabama led only 17–14.

The whole game turned now on the onside kick. Goss was on the field—and he got his second chance. A Tide player tipped the ball, as Goss recalled, "and it's coming straight to me. It is like slow motion. I jump and lay out for the ball. I catch it, curl up, and all of my teammates rush over and cover me up."

When Goss ran to the sidelines, a smiling Stallings was waiting. With a pat on the shoulder and a handshake, he said, "You're forgiven!"

Mulligans. It's a shame life doesn't emulate golf and that Outback Bowl and give us an occasional do-over. If you could go back and repair that relationship that meant so much to you, wouldn't you? If you got a second chance to take that job you passed up, wouldn't you? If you could take back those hateful words that you didn't really mean, wouldn't you?

God is a God of second chances—and third chances and fourth chances. No matter how many mistakes you make—and we all make a bunch—God will never give up on you.

Things could be worse. Suppose your errors were counted and published every day, like those of a baseball player.
—SOURCE UNKNOWN

▶ *That you make mistakes doesn't mean God will give up on you. He's a God of second chances.*

Mamas and Their Children

Read John 19:25–30.

"Meanwhile, standing near the cross of Jesus [was] his mother" (v. 25).

When he was thirteen, Bobby Humphrey disobeyed his mama—and got his start toward becoming one of the greatest running backs in Crimson Tide history, a two-time all-American, and an NFL star.

Marlene Humphrey did not want her son playing youth football, so young Bobby signed himself up secretly. In *Legends of Alabama Football*, Richard Scott explained, "To play football and keep his secret safe from mama, all Humphrey had to do was change out of his uniform after practice and get home before dark." But the first game ran late—after dark.

Humphrey said when he got home, his mama "had a limb, getting ready to spank me." But, Scott wrote, before Bobby's mama "could take her first swipe at her son's behind, Humphrey hid behind the trophy he brought home from the game." In his first game he had scored four touchdowns and earned the first of many trophies.

What was his mama's reaction?

"Normally I would have spanked him," she said. "But this time I saw the expression on his face, and I knew I was supposed to rejoice with him."

Her little boy was happy, so Marlene Humphrey was, too, even though she had to change her plans for her son.

Mamas do that sort of thing. Perhaps you can recall a time when your mother changed her plans for you. Jesus's mother, too, would have done anything for her son—including following him to his execution, an act of love and bravery, since her boy was condemned as an enemy of the Roman Empire.

But just as Mary, your mother, and Bobby Humphrey's mom would do anything for their offspring, so God will go to extraordinary lengths out of love for his children. After all, that was God on the cross at the foot of which Mary stood.

Everyone should find time to write and to go see their mother. I think that's healthy.
—BEAR BRYANT

Mamas often sacrifice for their children, but God, too, will take drastic measures for his children, including dying for them.

Playing with Pain

Read 2 Corinthians 1:3–7.

"Just as the sufferings of Christ are abundant for us, so also our consolation is abundant through Christ" (v. 5).

The stories surrounding Paul "Bear" Bryant are legendary, and some are downright mythical. None may be more impressive—yet true—than his performance against Tennessee in 1935, a game Alabama won 25–0.

Bryant played with a broken leg.

As Al Browning tells it in *Third Saturday in October*, Bryant was on crutches Friday afternoon with a splintered fibula cracked the previous Saturday against Mississippi State. The team physician took the cast off the night before the game and told Bryant he'd be able to dress out but not play. Before the game the next day, Coach Hank Crisp ended the pregame pep talk by saying, "I don't know about the rest of you, . . . but I know old 34 will be after them today." Bryant recalled they changed jersey numbers practically every week, and "I looked down to see what my jersey number was. There it was, as plain as day, old 34. . . . Coach [Frank] Thomas asked me if I could play. What could I have said? I just ran on out there."

Browning said *Atlanta Constitution* writer Ralph McGill was so skeptical that he asked to see the X-rays before he wrote his game story. As for the pain, Bryant reportedly said, "It was only a little bone."

You play with pain. Whether it's a car wreck that left you shattered, the end of a relationship that left you battered, or a loved one's death that left you tattered—pain finds you and challenges you to keep going.

So what are you to do when you're hit full-speed by the awful pain that seems to choke the very will to live out of you? Where is your consolation and comfort?

It's in almighty God, whose love will never fail. When life knocks you to your knees, you may just find you're closer to God than ever before.

It hurts up to a point, and then it doesn't get any worse.
—Ultramarathon runner Ann Trason

》 **When life hits you with pain, turn to God for comfort, consolation, and hope.**

Fear Factor

Read Matthew 14:22–33.

"When [Peter] noticed the strong wind, he became frightened, and beginning to sink, he cried out, 'Lord, save me!'" (v. 30).

Tackle Charlie Compton was a much-decorated hero of World War II who returned to Alabama in 1946 for his senior season. Yet when Coach Frank Thomas announced that the team was flying to a game for the first time (against Boston College), Compton promptly declared that he didn't fly on airplanes.

Alabama all-American halfback/quarterback Harry Gilmer told the story of the fearful flyer, recounted in Eli Gold's *Crimson Nation*. Gilmer said of Compton, he "was a very, very good player. . . . We thought he was a little wacky. . . . He was the leanest, best-conditioned athlete you have ever seen in your life."

Compton's feats of bravery and heroism in combat were legendary among his teammates, as was his toughness. He once "gashed his cheek during a play and proceeded to sew it up himself, right on the sidelines, so he could go back in and play." He also once came off the field and asked the manager for a pair of pliers, ostensibly for his cleats. Instead, he used the pliers to pull out a tooth so he could go back in.

Yet he refused to board a plane, telling Thomas, "Coach, I don't fly."

This war hero and rough, tough lineman was simply afraid.

Maybe—like Charlie Compton—flying scares you, too. Or speaking to the Rotary Club. Maybe elevator walls seem to close in on you. And let's not get started on spiders and snakes.

We all live in fear, and God knows this. About seventy-five passages in the Bible urge us not to be afraid. God isn't telling us to abandon our wariness of oncoming cars, big dogs with nasty dispositions, or flaming airplane engines. But he is reminding us that when we trust completely in him, we'll find peace that calms our fears.

God is greater than anything you fear.

> *Let me win. But if I cannot win,*
> *let me be brave in the attempt.*
> —SPECIAL OLYMPICS MOTTO

> **You have your own peculiar set of fears, but never let them paralyze you; remember that God is greater than anything you fear.**

The Prize

Read Philippians 3:10–16.

"I press on toward the goal for the prize of the heavenly call of God in Christ Jesus" (v. 14).

Lucille Long won the grand prize at an Alabama basketball game in 1916.

The prize was part of a promotional effort to spur interest in Crimson Tide basketball, which received little notice and less respect in the early days. Clyde Bolton said in *The Basketball Tide* that the sport suffered from a "lack of prominence in the town and on the campus." For instance, the *Tuscaloosa News* reported before the 1916 home opener that the game would end "at 7:15 o'clock in order to give time to those desiring to attend the glee club concert."

The players certainly didn't get much adulation. As Bolton put it, "Students in short pants throwing a ball at an iron hoop failed to captivate at least one faculty member." Three law students on the team had to take their books with them on every trip "because the dean of the law school didn't like his men in athletics," according to one team member.

So the sport needed some door prizes to spur interest. Just

what was the grand prize Long won, and how did she win it? She guessed the exact combined point total in the game, a 39– 34 Alabama loss to the Birmingham Athletic Club, and claimed a seven-pound box of candy.

Even the most modest among us can't help but be pleased by prizes and honors. They symbolize the approval and appreciation of others, whether it's an Employee of the Month trophy, a plaque for sales achievement, or a sign declaring yours the neighborhood's prettiest yard.

In your pursuit of personal achievement and accomplishment, be careful never to take your eyes off the greatest prize of all. It's one that won't rust, collect dust, or leave you wondering why you worked so hard to win it in the first place. It's eternal life, and it's yours through Jesus Christ.

A gold medal is a wonderful thing, but if you're not enough without it, you'll never be enough with it.
—JOHN CANDY IN *COOL RUNNINGS*

▷ **The greatest prize of all doesn't require competition to claim it; God has it ready to hand to you.**

DAY 12

An Unlikely Hero

Read 1 Samuel 16:1–13.

"Do not look on his appearance . . . for the LORD does not see as mortals see; . . . the LORD looks on the heart" (v. 7).

In the fourth quarter of the game on the third Saturday in October 1973, those in the press box in Legion Field were calling it the "best ever" Tennessee-Alabama game. The score was tied at 21. And then—incredibly—a baseball player turned the game around and became an unlikely hero.

According to Al Browning in *Third Saturday in October*, Robin Cary was a second baseman on the baseball team. He had good hands, so Coach Bear Bryant inserted him into the game with specific instructions: Catch a Tennessee punt. Well, Cary caught it all right. He then proceeded to run for sixty-four yards and a touchdown that blew the game wide open. Alabama rolled to a 42–21 win.

Cary's run didn't just surprise the crowd; the Tide players were stunned as well. "That little guy couldn't outrun his sister," recalled sophomore quarterback Robert Fraley. "But he sure outran a bunch of Volunteers in Birmingham." Mike Dubose, who was a junior defensive end that year, laughed that it "normally took [Cary] a day and a half to run forty yards."

Star quarterback Gary Rutledge summed it up: "That run by Robin Cary busted it open, no doubt about that." However unlikely, Robin Cary was the game's hero.

Most folks imagine a hero as someone who performs brave and dangerous feats that save or protect someone's life. So you figure that excludes you.

But ask your son about that when you show him how to bait a hook, or your daughter when you show up for her dance recital. Look into the eyes of those Little Leaguers you help coach.

Ask God about heroism when you're steady in your faith. For God, a hero is a person with the heart of a servant. God knows a heart truly devoted to him is the heart of a champion.

Heroes and cowards feel exactly the same fear;
heroes just act differently.
—LATE BOXING TRAINER CUS D'AMATO

> **God's heroes are the people who remain steady in their faith while serving others.**

DAY 13

Fathers and Sons

Read 2 Samuel 18:1–15, 31–33.

"[David] went up to the chamber over the gate, and wept; and as he went, he said, 'O my son Absalom, my son, my son Absalom! Would I had died instead of you, O Absalom, my son, my son!'" (v. 33).

Gabe Scott loved baseball. He starred for the Tide in the outfield through his senior season in 2005. During his time at Bama, however, he lost his desire to play and struggled to recover his love of the game.

That's because in 2002 he lost his dad, who died in September from a massive heart attack. As Richard D. Lee put it in his *Crimson White* article "Great Scott," "Ronnie Scott wasn't just [Gabe's] dad; he was his best friend."

Gabe agreed that when his dad died, he lost his best friend, and his mind turned to things other than baseball. "I always loved playing baseball. When [my dad] was gone, I knew that was something that connected me and him at a deeper level than other family members. Half of the game was lost."

But not all of it. Scott found support in his family back home in Lake Charles, Louisiana, and in his baseball family at

Alabama. He also found his love for the game again, and his senior season he starred for the twentieth-ranked Tide by leading the team in batting average, hits, and on-base percentage. He was named first-team all-SEC and second-team all-American.

For Scott, the season gave him a chance to reclaim his life and recover from the loss he had suffered.

You love your dad and make sure you eat dinner with him every Father's Day. Or maybe you don't talk to him if you can avoid it. You may not even know where he is and don't really care. But have you used your relationship with your father—loving, tempestuous, or nonexistent—to learn how to interact with your own son or daughter?

A model for the perfect relationship between a father and his children does exist: that of Jesus the Son and God the Father. You can look to their relationship for guidance and direction.

> *My dad was a huge influence on me. I imagine if he had put a wrench in my hand I would have been a great mechanic.*
> —PETE MARAVICH

> ⟩ **Fatherhood is a tough job, but a model for the father-child relationship is found in that between Jesus the Son and God the Father.**

Clothes Horse

Read Genesis 37:1–11.

"Israel loved Joseph more than all his children, because he was the son of his old age: and he made him a coat of many colors" (v. 3 KJV).

Do clothes make the football team?

"Despcription of Uniforms by Year" says that Alabama players wore crimson and white from the first season (1892) on, though the early players wore sweaters, not jerseys. A striped jersey was introduced in 1899, then the crimson jersey in 1900.

While the jerseys gradually evolved, so did the padding the players wore. By 1896 players had begun putting extra padding on their arms, and shoulder padding soon became common. Even into the 1920s, though, some players didn't wear helmets, and face masks weren't used until 1942.

Numbers were placed on the front of the jerseys in 1920, and players' names were added to the backs for the first time in 1981. The 1930 team sported white helmets with crimson markings, but not until 1957 did numbers first appear on the helmets. The crimson helmet made its first appearance in the 1960 Bluebonnet Bowl against Texas.

In 1980 the players wore those flashy white shoes for the first time, though in 1988 the Tide went back to black shoes.

Alabama's football uniform has undergone many changes over the decades and will probably continue to evolve. What has not changed, however, is that no matter what the Crimson Tide players are wearing, they win. For the Tide, clothes don't make the team.

Contemporary society seems to proclaim that it's all about the clothes. Buy that new suit or dress, those new shoes, and all the sparkling accessories, and you'll be a new person. The changes, though, are cosmetic; under those clothes, you're the same person. Consider Joseph running around in his fancy robe; he was still a spoiled tattletale.

A follower of Christ seeks to be like Jesus not through wearing special clothing, like a robe and sandals, but by developing inner beauty and serenity—whether the clothes are the sables of a king or the rags of a pauper.

> *You can't call [golf] a sport. You don't run, jump, you don't shoot, you don't pass. All you have to do is buy some clothes that don't match.*
> —FORMER MAJOR LEAGUER STEVE SAX

▶ **Where Jesus is concerned, clothes don't make the person; faith does.**

Choices

Read Deuteronomy 30:15–20.

"I have set before you life and death, blessings and curses. Choose life so that you and your descendents may live" *(v. 19).*

W hat in the world would make Mari Bayer travel all the way across the country in 2002 to go to college?

Among other things, God.

A native of San Jose, California, Bayer was a highly re-cruited gymnast out of high school and an unlikely candidate to ply her considerable talents for Alabama. Matt Scalici wrote in his *Crimson White* article "Tide's Bayer Has West Coast Flair" that when Bayer was "thinking about which college to attend, Alabama wasn't exactly the first name that came to mind." In fact, she was determined to stay in California. "My top two were Stanford and UCLA," she said.

So how did Bayer wind up an all-American in Tuscaloosa?

"I thought about it and prayed about it, and I ultimately re-alized that Alabama is where God wanted me to go," Bayer said.

Bayer's teammate and roommate, Meredith Laxton, said

Bayer is "a strong Christian," which is "definitely her motivation, and you can see her relationship with God out there. It's why she does what she does."

Mari Bayer's decision to come to Alabama was a radical one that forever changed her life. It took her far from her family and friends but gave her in return an all-SEC and all-American collegiate career.

Your life is the sum of the choices you've made. Your love of the Tide. Your spouse, or the absence of one. Your job. Your home. Even your pet. Your choices define you.

That includes faith—or the lack of it. God lets you choose, though he reminds you that his way is life and choosing against him is death.

Diehard Crimson Tide fans may argue that for Mari Bayer the choice between West Coast colleges and Alabama should have been obvious. In the case of your faith, you've been presented with life and death. It may seem obvious, but it's still up to you to choose life.

You're the only person who can decide where you want to go and how you're going to get there.

—TERRY BOWDEN

▶ **God gives you freedom of choice: life or death. Which will you choose?**

Glory!

Read Psalm 96.

"Ascribe to the LORD the glory due his name" (v. 8).

If one had to pinpoint when the true glory era of Alabama football began, it would be the moment when thirty-one-year-old Wallace Wade, the youngest Bama coach to date, arrived in Tuscaloosa in 1923 to take over as head coach."

So declared Eli Gold in *Crimson Nation.*

Wade coached the Crimson Tide for only eight seasons, but his record was a phenomenal 61–13–3. His teams won three national championships, including Alabama's first, and then Frank Thomas built on what Wade had started. Thomas's record at Alabama was a gaudy 115–24–7 with two national championships.

From 1955 through 1957, however, the Tide won only four games. The glory was gone—until Paul "Bear" Bryant answered the call and brought the glory back: six more national championships, thirteen SEC titles, and twenty-four consecutive bowl trips.

With the Bear's retirement in 1982 and his death in January 1983, Tide fans again knew the elusive nature of glory.

Since 1982 Alabama has won three SEC titles (1989, 1992, and 1999) and one national championship (in 1992 under Coach Gene Stallings). That would pass for glory days at many schools, but Alabama's tradition demands more.

The hard, cold truth is that any school—including Alabama—will have its down years. Glory on the gridiron is fleeting.

You'll never forget the play that was your moment of athletic glory. Or the night your civic club honored you. Your first (and last?) hole in one. Your first 10K race. Life has its moments of glory.

But the glory is gone with the moment, leaving precious memories but some pain, too, since you can never go back and do it again. Such is the way of any glory we attach to people and to earthly institutions and organizations. True glory should be given to only one: the Lord God almighty, creator of everything . . . including life's transient moments of glory.

The moment of victory is much too short to live for that and nothing else.
—TENNIS GREAT MARTINA NAVRATILOVA

> **Life's moments of glory are fleeting; true, eternal glory is the purview of almighty God.**

Southern Hospitality

Read 2 Kings 4:8–17.

"Let us make a small roof chamber with walls, and put there for him a bed, a table, a chair, and a lamp, so that he can stay there whenever he comes to us" (v. 10).

The folks who did the best job of recruiting Shaun Alexander to Alabama probably never even knew they were doing it.

Alexander was one of the Tide's greatest running backs ever. He set fifteen school records, was a unanimous choice for SEC Player of the Year his senior season (1999), and was all-SEC, academic all-SEC, and all-American.

But his coming to Alabama after high school wasn't a sure thing. After all, he was from Kentucky. As Wayne Atcheson put it in *Faith of the Crimson Tide,* "Shaun could have played football for Notre Dame. He could have played at Michigan, Ohio State, other Big Ten schools, and most any place he wanted."

So Alabama's rich football tradition, the opportunity to play in the Southeastern Conference where football is king, the warm weather—surely these helped tip the scales Alabama's way.

Well, actually, they didn't. So what was the key to Alexander's decision?

Of all things—according to Alexander—it was "the Southern hospitality. . . . The atmosphere of being around the people caused me to believe that, without a doubt, there was something special about the place. . . . [The people] were so friendly and enjoyed waiting on you and being hospitable. I really liked that, and it made quite an impression on me."

Southerners are deservedly famous for their hospitality. Down South, warmth and genuineness seem genetic. You open your home to the neighborhood kids, to your friends, to the stranger whose car broke down in the rain, to the stray cat that showed up hungry and hollering. You even let family members overstay their welcome without grumbling.

Your hospitality is a sign of your loving and generous nature, a touch of the divine in you. God, too, is a gracious host, and one day he will open the doors of his home for you— and never ask you to leave.

> *Being raised in the South means growing up on a diet of southern hospitality and a dose of football every weekend.*
> —JILL ARRINGTON

➤ **Hospitality is an outward sign of the inward loving and generous nature of the host.**

Necessary Things

Read Luke 18:18–25.

"There is still one thing lacking. Sell all that you own and distribute the money to the poor, and you will have treasure in heaven; then come, follow me" (v. 22).

On November 11, 1892, Alabama played its first-ever football game.

From the first, the sport so popular in the North drew the attention of the press. In *The Crimson Tide* Clyde Bolton said the *Birmingham Daily News* reported on that first game, noting in an advance story that at three o'clock sharp at "the baseball park," "Alabama's 'famous' team would meet a 'picked eleven from Professor Taylor's and the High School.'" The effervescent sportswriter declared this new game of football to be "the great amateur game of America, which is played by gentlemen."

The opponent was Birmingham High School, and in its report on the game, the *Daily News* said, "The school team was made up of a handsome crowd of boys, but as soon as they came out on the grounds, every one knew they were too light to cope with their heavy antagonists, and that no matter how quick their play, they must succumb to the cadets' strength."

The story was colorful, but it omitted details about the game—including the score and how the teams scored. In other words, the writer filled his story with fluff and omitted practically everything necessary to a good story about the game.

It's possible to omit the necessary things in life, too. We clutter our lives with things, with trinkets, with toys; we surround ourselves with stuff, little of which brings more than momentary satisfaction.

Yes, that boat, those cars, that house, even that big ol' riding lawn mower and that high-definition plasma TV are nice. But what really matters in life is not ephemeral wealth and the replaceable things it buys but lasting love and the irreplaceable people you give it to and receive it from, including Jesus.

It's all about the love; love is the necessary thing.

And, by the way, Alabama won that first game 56–0.

From what we get, we can make a living; what we give, however, makes a life.
—Arthur Ashe

≫ **Material wealth and possessions can clutter a life, but they can never fill it.**

Getting No Respect

Read Mark 8:31–38.

*"He began to teach them that the Son of Man must un-
dergo great suffering, and be rejected by the elders, the
chief priests, and the scribes, and be killed" (v. 31).*

Talk about not getting any respect.

A group of racquetball players at Alabama got together in
the summer of 2003 and established the school's first competi-
tive racquetball team, a club sport. All the players did in the
team's first year of existence was go undefeated and win the
2004 national championship. According to the article "UA
Wins," more than forty schools competed for that title, including some familiar names such as Auburn, Penn State, Texas,
North Carolina, Ohio State, and Arizona.

The Alabama team was young: six freshmen, one sophomore, and one junior. Yet they traveled all the way to California
and claimed the title, with five of the freshmen making all-
American.

It may well have been the splashiest debut of any sports
team in Alabama history.

So what happened? The university cut its financial support

of the club in half. The team promptly responded with a second straight national championship.

Sophomore Agustin Tristan voiced the team's opinion about the lack of respect. "We don't get the recognition that I think we should deserve from the University," he told the *Crimson White*'s Dennis Pillion for the article "Still Perfect." "Since we're just a club sport, they don't care about us. This year, they only gave us $1,000 for the whole year, which is nothing. That's only like three plane tickets."

Rodney Dangerfield made a good living as a comedian with a repertoire that was really only countless variations on one punch line: "I don't get no respect." Dangerfield was successful because he struck a chord with his audience. No one wants to be perceived by others as being worthy of only "three plane tickets." You want the respect, honor, esteem, and regard you feel you've earned.

Probably more often than not, you don't get it; but that doesn't stop you from succeeding. Anyway, don't feel too bad; you're in good company. Look how they treated Jesus.

Play for your own self-respect
and the respect of your teammates.
—Vanderbilt coach Dan McGugin

➤ **You may not get the respect you deserve, but dare to succeed anyway.**

In the Beginning

Read Genesis 1:1–31; 2:1–3.

"God saw everything that he had made, and indeed, it was very good" (v. 1:31).

He was the beginning of modern football.

In the beginning the forward pass was the "vestige of the few, far, and in-between," a "necessary evil" for college football coaches, according to Richard Scott in *Legends of Alabama Football.*

Then along came an Alabama football player who changed everything. Scott said we find him back there in the 1930s "at the place where passing became more than an occasional deception or novelty act and receivers became more than blockers. At the place where passing became a reality and receivers became dangerous weapons." He was, Scott wrote, "arguably the best, or at least the most innovative receiver in the history of football."

He was Alabama's own Don Hutson. In 1934 he was all-SEC and all-American, and in the 1935 Rose Bowl against Stanford, he caught six passes for 165 yards and two touchdowns to lead the Crimson Tide to their fourth national championship.

When he died in 1997, he still held ten NFL and eighteen team records. And remember, he played pro football in the 1940s.

Tony Canadeo, a teammate of Hutson's with the Green Bay Packers, told Scott, "To me, he made the passing game what it is today."

In the beginning of modern football, there was Don Hutson.

Every morning when you first awake, you get a gift from God: a new beginning. The day lies before you expectant and pristine. You can use it to pay a debt, start a new relationship, replace a burned-out light bulb, tell your family you love them, chase a dream, solve a nagging problem, or right old wrongs. Or not.

God simply provides the gift. How you use it is up to you. People often talk wistfully about starting over or making a new beginning. God gives you that chance with the dawning of every new day.

> *The most important key to achieving great*
> *success is to decide upon your goal and launch,*
> *get started, take action, move.*
> —JOHN WOODEN

> ⟫ **Every dawn is not just a new day; it is a precious**
> **chance to begin anew.**

Party Time

Read Exodus 14:26–31; 15:19–21.

"The prophet Miriam, Aaron's sister, took a tambourine in her hand; and all the women went out after her with tambourines and with dancing" (v. 15:20).

One writer/professor called Alabama's 20–19 win over Washington in the 1926 Rose Bowl "the most significant event in Southern football history," according to Eli Gold in *Crimson Nation*.

The bowl game was Alabama's first, and the win clinched the Crimson Tide's first national title. Years later Coach Wallace Wade, who by then had two more national titles to his credit, said, "I still regard the 1926 Alabama-Washington game as the most spectacular, exciting, and dramatic college football game in Alabama history."

But the win was not just for one team from Tuscaloosa. The whole South joined the Alabama faithful in celebrating. Winthrop University Professor Andrew Doyle said that the win by the first southern team ever to participate in the Rose Bowl "was a sublime tonic for southerners who were buffeted by a legacy of defeat, military defeat, a legacy of poverty, and a legacy of isolation from the American political and cultural mainstream."

The party was on. Gold wrote, "As the squad returned home from California . . . they were cheered, paraded, and celebrated at every stop." A thousand Tulane students cheered them when they came through New Orleans. When the victors finally arrived in Tuscaloosa, "the whole town had already begun celebrating a festive holiday, complete with parades and parties."

Invite some friends over, throw some burgers and hot dogs on the grill, turn on the game on TV, pull out the salsa and chips, and you've got a party. It doesn't even have to be game day; any old excuse will do. All you need is a sense that life is pretty good right now.

Jesus turns all of life into a celebration. No matter what tragedies or setbacks may be in store, the heart given to Jesus will still find joy in living. The party never stops when a life is celebrated with Jesus!

Aim high and celebrate that!
—MARATHON RUNNER BILL RODGERS

▷ **With Jesus, life is one big party, a celebration of victory and joy.**

DAY 22

Working for It

Read John 15:12–17.

"You did not choose me but I chose you. And I appointed you to go and bear fruit, fruit that will last" (v. 16).

When school let out in the summer of 2004, junior Stephanie VanBrakle didn't head for the beach or home to hang out with her friends. She went to work.

She spent the summer playing softball for the Brakettes, a women's softball team from Connecticut. Why? To be a better softball player for the Crimson Tide.

According to Jessie Patterson's *Crimson White* article "Van-Brakle Helps Team to 11–0 Start," VanBrakle "worked a lot harder over the summer by playing with a women's team. . . . I worked on mental stuff. . . . I learned a new riseball grip. My pitching has come around a lot from last year. I've tried to improve everything."

Did the work pay off? Head coach Patrick Murphy didn't know what VanBrakle had been up to over the break, but he noticed a difference in her performance immediately. "I could tell she was in better shape," he said. "She committed herself to the team."

The real proof was in VanBrakle's junior season, in 2005. She was named all-American after posting a sparkling 34–7 record with a 1.34 ERA. In the College World Series against DePaul, she struck out seventeen, a school record. The team went 63–15, the second-most wins in school history, and won the SEC tournament.

Stephanie VanBrakle succeeded because of her hard work.

Funny thing about all these labor-saving devices like cell phones, fax machines, and laptop computers: We're working longer and harder than ever. Even retirees are working more these days. Your work defines you perhaps more than any other aspect of your life. But there's a workforce you're part of that doesn't show up in any Labor Department statistics or IRS records.

You're part of God's staff. You are charged with the awesome responsibility of spreading as much of his love as possible. The hours are awful—24/7—but the benefits are out of this world.

Sacrifice. Work. Self-discipline. I teach these things, and my boys don't forget them when they leave.

—BEAR BRYANT

▶ **God has a job for you: spreading his love around. Get to work!**

Jumping for Joy

Read Luke 6:20–26.

"Rejoice in that day and leap for joy, for surely your reward is great in heaven" (v. 23).

Eli Gold wrote in *Crimson Nation*, "Harry Gilmer was absolutely the star of his era [1944–47] and arguably the best all-around, four-year player Bama has ever had."

One thing is for sure: The University of Alabama will never see the likes of Harry Gilmer again. It wasn't just the statistics, including fifty-two career touchdowns, still a school record. It wasn't just his versatility, though in 1946 Gilmer was the team leader in both passing and rushing and in interceptions, punt returns, and kickoff returns.

The primary reason Alabama fans won't see Gilmer's equal again is that nobody throws the ball the way he did—nor is anyone likely to. He was small, so he developed a unique style to see and throw over the bigger linemen: He jumped. Gilmer took the snap from center, stepped back, jumped up, and then threw the ball.

How good was he despite this unorthodox style? Legendary sportswriter Grantland Rice called Gilmer "the greatest college passer I ever saw." In 1945 Gilmer was the SEC's Most Valuable Player, first-team all-American, and Most Valuable Player in the Rose Bowl, leading Alabama to a 34–14 trouncing of favored Southern Cal.

He did all of that by jumping high in the air and then sending the ball flying downfield, a style uniquely his own.

You're probably a pretty good jumper yourself when Alabama scores against Tennessee, LSU, or Auburn. You just can't help it. It's like your feet and your seat have suddenly become magnets that repel each other. The sad part is that you always come back down to earth, the moment of exultation passing.

But what if you could jump for joy all the time? Not literally, of course; you'd pass out from exhaustion. But figuratively, with your heart aglow and joyous even when life is most difficult?

That's the way you are to live, Jesus said: always jumping for joy.

I would have thought that the knowledge that you are going to be leapt upon by half-a-dozen congratulatory, but sweaty teammates would be inducement not to score a goal.
—Broadcaster Arthur Marshall

> **Unbridled joy can send you jumping all over the place, and Jesus said such exultation should not be something rare but a way of life.**

Blind Justice

Read Micah 6:6–8.

"He has told you, O mortal, what is good; and what does the LORD *require of you but to do justice, and to love kindness, and to walk humbly with your God?" (v. 8).*

Let's just state the plain, blunt truth up front: Alabama was robbed of the 1977 national championship.

The Tide rolled to a 10–1 record and the SEC championship. The only loss was to Nebraska, 31–24, in the second game of the season. With a schedule that took on all comers, Bama defeated Georgia, Southern Cal, Tennessee, LSU, Miami, and Auburn along the way.

This was a talented team led by senior all-American wide receiver Ozzie Newsome and all-SEC players (in addition to Newsome) Jim Bunch, tackle; Johnny Davis, the power fullback who was the heart of the wishbone; defensive back Mike Kramer; and center Dwight Stephenson. Bunch and Stephenson would be all-Americans in 1979.

Alabama finished the season ranked third in the nation, behind top-ranked Texas and Ohio State. The Tide then proceeded to demolish Woody Hayes and Ohio State 35–6 in the

Sugar Bowl as quarterback Jeff Rutledge threw two touchdown passes and was the game's MVP.

The Tide faithful had further cause for jubilation when word came in from Dallas and the Cotton Bowl: Notre Dame had whipped Texas 38–10. The national championship apparently was Alabama's.

But the pollsters jumped the Fighting Irish over Alabama and awarded Notre Dame the title. The Tide was robbed!

Where's the justice when cars fly past you just as a state trooper pulls you over? When a con artist swindles an elderly neighbor? When crooked politicians treat your tax dollars as their personal slush fund? When children starve?

Justice isn't blind; it's random—or so it seems. Maybe you can't rid the world of injustice, but you can establish justice for all in the corner where you live. God expects you to be a just person, and he promises you justice in return. The justice you receive from God depends on the justice you give others.

> *The strong take from the weak, and the smart*
> *take from the strong.*
> —Former Princeton basketball coach Pete Carril

>> **The justice you receive from God will depend on the justice you give to others.**

DAY 25

Comeback Kids

Read Acts 9:1–22.

"All who heard him were amazed and said, 'Is this not the man who made havoc in Jerusalem among those who invoked this name?'" (v. 21).

It was the greatest comeback in the history of the University of Alabama's women's basketball program, and one of the greatest in any sport.

In December 2001 the Crimson Tide was simply getting worn out by South Alabama. After shooting a woeful 26 percent, Alabama trailed at halftime 41–21 and fell behind by as many as twenty-four points in the last half. South Alabama seemingly had the game wrapped up with a 61–44 lead and only 6:31 left to play.

Yet Bama coach Rick Moody told Micah Lewter of *The Crimson White*, "I never stopped believing we were going to win." Moody transformed his faint hopes into a strategy. "I told our players, 'You can't come back on the offensive end. You have to come back on the defensive end.'" And so they did. Incredibly, Alabama did not allow South Alabama to score another point.

Equally incredibly, the Alabama women proceeded to score

nineteen straight points. Senior point guard Shondra Johnson got loose for a lay-up with only sixteen seconds left and then added a free throw to cap the unbelievable run. Alabama won 63–61. Over the last 10:12 of the game, the Tide outscored South Alabama 23–3 to pull off a comeback for the ages.

You've probably had to pull off a comeback of your own. Maybe financial problems suffocated you. A serious illness put you on the sidelines. Or you had to beat an addiction. Life is a series of victories and defeats. Winning isn't about avoiding defeat; it's about getting back up to compete again.

You're never too far behind, and it's never too late in life's game for Jesus to lead you to victory. As with the Alabama women against South Alabama, and as with Saul in his journey to faith, it's not how you start that counts; it's how you finish.

Turn a setback into a comeback.
—Football coach Billy Brewer

In life, victory is truly a matter of how you finish and whether you finish with Jesus at your side.

Juggernaut

Read Revelation 20.

"Fire came down from heaven and consumed them. And the devil who had deceived them was thrown into the lake of fire and sulfur, where the beast and the false prophet were" (vv. 9–10).

W e're gonna drill Tennessee like an enraged wild boar." So said Doug Layton, the color analyst on the Alabama Radio Network, before the Alabama-Tennessee game of 1986, according to Al Browning's *Third Saturday in October.*

Layton had a bit of the prophet in him. In one of the most humiliating afternoons in University of Tennessee football history, the Tide crushed Tennessee 56–28, decisively ending a four-game losing streak to the Volunteers.

Sophomore tailback Bobby Humphrey ran for three touchdowns and 217 yards on twenty-seven carries, only sixteen yards short of the school record set by Bobby Marlow against Auburn in 1951. But Humphrey had plenty of help as the Crimson Tide rolled up 457 yards rushing, scoring the most points against Tennessee since Duke defeated them 70–0 in 1893. Alabama had the ball ten times and scored eight touchdowns.

The Tide thoroughly humiliated the Volunteer defense by running the same play—a power sweep by the tailback—twenty-seven times.

Alabama led 21–0 after the first quarter and 42–14 at halftime. Quite simply, the 7–0 Tide massacred the 2–4 Volunteers. That afternoon in Knoxville, the Bama offense was a juggernaut that could barely be slowed down, let alone stopped, scoring on drives of 74, 43, 12, 74, 62, 48, 80, and 56 yards.

Maybe your experience with a juggernaut involved a game against a team full of college prospects, a league tennis match against a former college player, or your presentation for the project you knew didn't stand a chance. Whatever it was, you've been slam-dunked before.

Being part of a juggernaut is certainly more fun than being in the way of one. Just ask the 1986 Volunteers. Or consider the forces of evil aligned against God. They'll be trounced in the most decisive victory and defeat of all time. You sure want to be on the winning side in that one.

I'd never been to a mercy killing before.
—New Orleans basketball coach Benny Dees
after a 101–76 loss to Alabama

The most lopsided victory in all of history is a sure thing: God's ultimate triumph over evil.

Stinking to High Heaven

Read John 11:1–16, 38–44.

"Martha, the sister of the dead man, said to him, 'Lord, already there is a stench because he has been dead four days.' Jesus said to her, 'Did I not tell you that if you believed, you would see the glory of God?'" (vv. 39–40).

One particular night the Alabama men's basketball team really stunk up the gym, but not because of the way they played.

As Jim Homer, the first Alabama basketball player to score three hundred points in a season, told it in Clyde Bolton's *The Basketball Tide*, Alabama played Mississippi State in the late 1940s in an old Quonset hut that passed for the Bulldog gymnasium. The facility was so inadequate that at halftime the players had to go outside to use the rest room.

The trip promptly turned into a disgusting disaster. Homer said, "What we didn't know was that there was an open sewer line out there. Three of us fell into that thing."

They were a revolting sight, bearing an even more repulsive smell, when they returned to the gym still wearing the residue from their luckless fall. What to do? "Coach Hank [Crisp] saw us and yelled, 'Get them into the shower!' We got in, clothes, shoes, and all." The shower got the players clean, but it sure didn't make them more comfortable. Homer said, "I'll never forget playing that entire second half soaking wet."

Fortunately, the Tide players didn't perform as badly as they smelled or felt. Squishy shoes, pungent uniforms, and all, they won the game.

It's a smelly world we live in. Grease traps, full garbage cans on a summer day, dirty sneakers, rotten meat—they stink. It's also an aromatic world we live in. Roses, coffee percolating, freshly laundered clothes, your loved one's body spray—they intoxicate.

Doesn't death stink, too, literally and metaphorically? Literally—think road kill. Metaphorically—think life's end. But once Jesus proved himself to be the Lord over death as well as life, death no longer stank to high heaven but became instead the way to high heaven. That makes it a sweet fragrance indeed.

Forget about sports as a profession. Sports make ya grunt and smell. See, be a thinker, not a stinker.
—APOLLO CREED IN *ROCKY*

▶ **Because of Jesus, rather than stinking to high heaven, death is the way to high heaven.**

Burying the Hatchet

Read 2 Corinthians 5:16–21.

"All this is from God, who reconciled us to himself through Christ, and has given us the ministry of reconciliation"
(v. 18).

On the morning of the final Alabama football game of the 1948 season, an unusual, highly symbolic, and important ceremony took place. As Clyde Bolton told it in *The Crimson Tide,* the presidents of the student bodies of Alabama and Auburn met, "dug a hole in the ground in Woodrow Wilson Park [in Birmingham], tossed a hatchet in, and buried it."

This literal burying of the hatchet symbolized the figurative burying that was to take place later that day when Alabama and Auburn met in a football game for the first time since 1907. Bolton said the series had been dropped because of a dispute over how many players Auburn could suit up, how much expense money Auburn was to receive, and whether a southern or an eastern umpire should be brought in. By the time the disputes were resolved, October had arrived and the schedules were made. The series simply lapsed.

Over the years the schools had attempted several times,

without success, to resume the series. Eventually politicians got involved. Pressured by the state legislature, the schools agreed to play in Birmingham.

Remember that buddy you used to go fishing with? That friend you used to roam the mall with? The one who introduced you to sushi? Remember the person who was so special you thought he or she might be "the one"? And now you don't even speak because of something—who remembers exactly?— one of you did.

Jesus told us to forgive others, which is easier said than done. But reconciling with others makes life richer and fuller. Holding a grudge is a way to self-destruction. Kissing and making up is a way of life.

The Alabama-Auburn hatchet remains buried, and the game is by far the state's number-one sports attraction today. And, oh, yes. Alabama won that renewal game in 1948, 55–0.

Life is short, so don't waste any of it carrying around a load of bitterness. It only sours your life, and the world won't pay any attention anyway.
—Pat Dye

▸ **Making up with others frees you from your past, turning you loose to get on with your richer, fuller future.**

DAY 29

Things That Never Change

Read Hebrews 13:5–16.

"Jesus Christ is the same yesterday and today and forever"
(v. 8).

What game is this?

The helmet was a piece of leather with cotton under it. The ball was the shape of a watermelon, too big to hold in your hand and pass. A player might have pads, but only if he provided them himself.

Hiding the ball under a jersey. A player dressed in civilian clothes hiding in the crowd until the play begins. Spectators rushing onto the field and getting in the players' way or throwing sticks and rocks at the opposing players during the game. Players dragging ball carriers forward. Linemen holding hands and jumping to the right or the left right before a play began. Automobiles lighting up the playing field.

What game is this?

According to Clyde Bolton in *The Crimson Tide,* this was the wild and woolly game of college football in its early days, the 1890s and the turn of the century. Largely unregulated and unsophisticated, with no forward pass, it was a game we would barely recognize today.

Thank goodness, we might say. Given the symmetry, the excitement, the passion, and the sheer spectacle that surround today's college games, few, if any, Alabama fans would long for the days when handles were sewn into the uniforms of ball carriers to make them easier to toss.

Like everything else, football has changed. Think back to when you were sixteen. Much that's routine in your life now wasn't even in it then—possibly everything from computers and CDs to cell phones and George Foreman grills.

Have you ever found yourself bewildered by the rapid pace of change? Casting about for something to hold on to that will always be the same, that will always be there when you need it? Is there anything like that?

Indeed there is: Jesus Christ, the same today, the same forever, always dependable, always loving you. Some things never change, thank God!

I'm not too proud to change. I like to win too much.
—BOBBY BOWDEN

> **In our ever-changing and bewildering world, Jesus is the same forever; his love for you will never change.**

The Funeral

Read Romans 6:3–11.

"If we have died with Christ, we believe that we will also live with him" (v. 8).

For sixty miles people are lined up along the highway crying. They were just bawling their eyes out on the overpass! I said, man, this is bigger than I ever imagined!"

That's the way Alabama defensive back Jeremiah Castille described what was indeed the biggest funeral the state of Alabama has ever seen, according to Eli Gold in *Crimson Nation*. On January 28, 1983, Alabama buried the Bear.

Paul "Bear" Bryant had quite a send-off, the funeral of a true hero. Thousands of mourners lined I-59 between Tuscaloosa and Birmingham, along which the funeral procession made its solemn journey. A radio station devoted the entire day to covering the funeral live, with reporters talking to politicians and celebrities who had come to pay their respects. TV stations also carried the funeral live. Gold wrote, "Some ten thousand people jammed outside the church in Birmingham to listen to the service on the loudspeakers. . . . The state of Alabama ground to a halt." On this one day, Gold said,

Auburn or Alabama didn't matter. "Everyone mourned Coach Bryant."

Bryant was buried in Birmingham in Elmwood Cemetery. His gravesite is easily found: A crimson line leads from the cemetery entrance to the great coach's final resting place.

Chances are you won't get that kind of send-off, one usually reserved for the likes of kings, popes, presidents—and Bear Bryant. Still, you want a good funeral.

But have you ever been to a memorial where everyone struggled to say something nice about the not-so-dearly departed? Or one that seems just an acknowledgment that death is the end of all hope? Sad, isn't it?

Exactly what makes a good funeral, one where people laugh and love amid their tears? Jesus does. His presence transforms a mourning of death into a celebration of life.

> *Always go to other people's funerals;*
> *otherwise, they won't come to yours.*
> —YOGI BERRA

> *Jesus's presence transforms a funeral from a lamenting of death to a celebration of life.*

The Right Person for the Job

Read Matthew 26:47–50; 27:1–10.

"The betrayer had given them a sign, saying, 'The one I will kiss is the man; arrest him.' At once he came up to Jesus and said, 'Greetings, Rabbi!' and kissed him" (vv. 48–49).

A horse-racing writer from Cleveland?

What in the world was Dr. George Hutcheson Denny, president of the University of Alabama, thinking when he named the Tide's new head football coach in 1919? If ever there was a man who was an unlikely choice to coach college football, it was Xen Scott, who succeeded Thomas Kelley after typhoid fever forced Kelley to retire.

Scott had never coached, was a sportswriter who covered four-legged athletes, and—worst of all for the Crimson Tide faithful—was a Yankee from Ohio. Even his disposition worked against him. Gold said in *Crimson Nation*, "Scott was an incredibly easygoing man," and "many people doubted he would be able to instill the discipline necessary to win."

No experience and a nice man, too? He had no chance.

But Scott made believers out of those who doubted him.

His first team got the Tide back on track after the year off in 1918 because of World War I by rolling to an 8–1 record. The 1920 team was even better at 10–1. Scott retired after the 1922 season because of his health. He had four winning seasons and compiled a record of 29–9–3, making him, at the time, Alabama's winningest coach ever.

Xen Scott was indeed the right man for the job.

How many career changes have you made? Like many people, you chase the job that gives you not just financial rewards but also some personal satisfaction and sense of accomplishment. You want a profession that uses your abilities, that you enjoy, that gives you a sense of contributing to something bigger than yourself.

God, too, wants you in the right job. Even Judas was the right man for what God needed to be done. To do his work, God gave you abilities, talents, and passions. Do what you do best and what you love—just do it for God.

A winner is someone who recognizes his God-given talents, works to develop them into skills, and uses these skills to accomplish his goals.
—LARRY BIRD

▷ **God has a job for you, one for which he has given you particular talents, abilities, and passions.**

A Family Affair

Read Mark 3:31–35.

*"Here are my mother and my brothers! Whoever does
the will of God is my brother and sister and mother"*
(vv. 34–35).

On April 11, 2005, Alabama women's golf coach Betty
Palmer caught some folks by surprise when she announced
her retirement after seventeen years at the Capstone.

She left at the top of her game, exiting with a list of achievements that included eight team tournament titles, seven
NCAA regional appearances, eleven all-SEC golfers, three all-
Americans, two NCAA individual tournament qualifiers, and
one SEC Scholar-Athlete of the Year.

So why would Palmer, the winningest coach in Alabama
women's golf history, suddenly quit when coaches are usually
forced out rather than leaving on their own terms? For her
family.

Palmer admitted to Jessie Patterson of the *Crimson White*,
in "Palmer Retires," that the decision was a tough one because
some goals weren't accomplished. But her husband and her
daughter, Katie, then twelve, came first. Palmer said her

husband's new teaching job at Jacksonville State University coupled with her "being gone eighty to one hundred days out of the year" left daughter Katie "out in the cold. We factored everything in, and it just didn't make sense. I've got one child and one shot at this." So she decided the whole family needed to move to Jacksonville; that meant giving up her career at Alabama.

Simply put, Betty Palmer's family came in ahead of her personal goals.

Some wit said families are like fudge, mostly sweet with a few nuts. You can probably call the names of your sweetest relatives, whom you cherish, and of the nutty ones, too. Like it or not, you have a family, and that's God's doing. God cherishes the family so much that he lived in one—and then redefined the family as all of his followers rather than as an accident of birth.

What a startling and wonderful thought: You have family members you don't even know, who stand ready to love you just because you're part of God's family.

Football has affected my entire family's lifestyle. My little boy can't go to bed unless we give him a two-minute warning.
—Coach Dick Vermeil

>> **Family, for the followers of Jesus, comes not from a shared ancestry but from a shared faith.**

David versus Goliath: Sugar Bowl Style

Read 1 Samuel 17:17–51.

"This very day the Lord *will deliver you into my hand"*
(v. 46).

We're 13 and 0 and still ain't played nobody."

That's the grammatically challenged sign defensive end John Copeland saw when Alabama arrived in New Orleans for the 1993 Sugar Bowl, according to Eli Gold in *Crimson Nation.* The sign was an expression of the general disdain in which the undefeated Crimson Tide was held—especially by their opposition, the Miami Hurricanes.

The national championship was on the line, but the talking heads had pretty much conceded the victory to the Canes. In speaking of the Tide, ESPN's Leo Corso had declared, "I know they're 10–0, but I just don't get it." Tide quarterback Jay Barker told Gold he read "a story in the paper that compared the upcoming game to a David and Goliath battle. 'I don't know if they ever read the Word,' Barker laughed. 'But David won that battle.'"

And the "David" dressed in crimson and white won this match-up about as convincingly as the youngest son of Jesse won his crucial battle long ago. Alabama blasted Miami and their Heisman Trophy winner Gino Torretta 34–13. The game was over early. As Copeland put it, "In the second quarter, I saw Torretta look over at me, and he froze for a second. I saw fear."

You probably don't gird your loins, pick up a slingshot, and go out to battle ill-tempered giants. You do, however, fight each day to make some economic and social progress. Armed only with your pluck, your knowledge, your wits, and your hustle, in many ways you are an underdog. You need all the weapons you can muster.

How about using the one David had: the conviction that when he tackled opposition of any size, he would prevail because God was with him. If you do everything for God's glory, you'll be doing it with God's assistance. Who's the underdog then?

> *Always remember that Goliath was*
> *a forty-point favorite over Little David.*
> —SHUG JORDAN

▷ **With God on your side, you will prevail.**

Fired Up

Read Hebrews 3:12–19.

"Exhort one another every day, as long as it is called 'today,' so that none of you may be hardened by the deceitfulness of sin" (v. 13).

They "are expected to schedule their classes around the practice times determined by the coach. In addition to practice time, [they] are required to attend weight-lifting and aerobics sessions."

What tough, demanding sport is this referring to? According to "Cheerleaders: General Information," it's cheerleading.

Cheerleaders at the University of Alabama aren't new. As Eli Gold noted in *Crimson Nation,* a type of cheerleader was introduced in the late 1890s. These were women students called "sponsors," though they didn't garner much respect. A newspaper article of the time said they were "society belles and school girls" who wore the school colors and applauded on cue without really knowing anything about football.

Aerobics, weightlifting, practices—today's Alabama cheerleaders are anything but "society belles" who merely show up in school colors, ignorant of the game. As one of Alabama's most famous former cheerleaders—Emmy Award–winning actress Sela Ward—said in "Smack Dab in the Middle of It All," "Bama football was as serious as religion, and to be a cheerleader, down on the field, smack dab in the middle of it all, was a privilege of the highest order!"

Ward fired up the Tide faithful from the Bama sidelines in the 1970s and said that "a southern gal from Mississippi" wound up in Hollywood "as a direct result of having been a cheerleader for Alabama."

It's been a long, hard day. The couch is calling, but your desk is stacked with work. You're exhausted. And suddenly they show up: your personal cheerleading team. They dance, cheer, shout, wave pompoms, and exhort you to more and greater effort. They fire you up. That would work, wouldn't it? If only . . .

But you do have just such a squad in your faith life: your fellow Christians. They come in teams—called churches—and they are exhorters who keep each other "in the game" that is faith. Christians are cheerleaders for God—and for God's team.

A cheerleader is a dreamer that never gives up.
—Source unknown

> **In the people of your church, you have your own set of cheerleaders to urge you to greater faithfulness.**

Attitude Check

Read Proverbs 6:12–23.

"A scoundrel and a villain goes around with crooked speech, winking the eyes, shuffling the feet, pointing the fingers, with perverted mind devising evil, continually sowing discord" (vv. 12–14).

A teammate called him "the perfect quarterback." Yet, as Richard Scott pointed out in *Legends of Alabama Football*, his name isn't found anywhere in the Alabama football media guide under any of the major school passing records such as attempts, completions, yardage, touchdowns, and completion percentage.

So who was this "perfect" quarterback, and why was he so great?

He was Pat Trammell—and he was great because he won. In his three seasons as the starter, 1959–61, the Tide was 26–2–4. His senior season he led Bear Bryant's first recruits to an 11–0 record and the national and SEC championships.

What made him so good at his job?

Legendary Alabama linebacker Lee Roy Jordan, a teammate all three years Trammell started, knows exactly what it was. "It was attitude," he said. "He didn't pass too good, he didn't run too good, all he did was win. . . . Whatever we needed, he got a little more than we needed. He had that tough mental attitude that said we can do anything."

Trammell maintained that tough, winning attitude until the untimely end of his life. In December 1968, Dr. Pat Trammell died of cancer. He told Bryant, "Coach, don't feel too sorry for me. I have had a wonderful twenty-nine years."

You can fuss because your house is not as big as some, because a coworker talks too much, or because you have to take pills every day. Or you can appreciate your home for giving you warmth and shelter, the coworker for lively conversation, and the medicine for keeping you at least reasonably healthy. The difference is not facts but attitude.

Life can be either endured or enjoyed, suffered or celebrated. The difference lies largely in your attitude. Good or bad, the one you adopt goes a long way toward determining the quality of your life.

I became an optimist when I discovered that I wasn't going to win any more games by being anything else.
—BASEBALL MANAGER EARL WEAVER

▷ **Your attitude determines more than your mood; it shapes the kind of person you are.**

Peacemongers

Read Hebrews 12:14–17.

"Pursue peace with everyone, and the holiness without which no one will see the Lord" (v. 14).

The Alabama basketball team once got into a brawl with the opposition—before the game started.

As Clyde Bolton recounted in *The Basketball Tide*, Kentucky's Adolph Rupp liked to have his subs stand at midcourt and watch the opposition warm up, an intimidating tactic. In 1955 Alabama coach Johnny Dee decided to return the favor, "to fight glare with glare," so he dispatched his subs "to the center line to disdainfully check out the Wildcats."

With the players in such close proximity, glares and stares soon turned to words, and words soon turned to blows. Bolton wrote, "Soon basketball players were swinging away, and there was a pileup in the middle of the floor." It took state troopers to restore order.

Not much real damage was done, though Tide center Jim Bogan suffered a bite on his chest and noted how weird it was "to lie there with your arms pinned down while a guy bites on you, and you watching him do it." Coach Dee was careful to protect his starters. Leon Marlaire recalled, "We were all trying to get in it, but Coach Dee had all the starters on the bench, and he was saying, 'You can't get in it! You just sit there!'"

Perhaps you've never been in a barroom brawl or a public brouhaha, but maybe like the Tide team of 1955 you retaliated when you got one smart remark too many. Or maybe you and your spouse or your teenager get into it occasionally, shouting and saying unkind things. Road rage may be a part of your life, too.

While we may live in a more belligerent, confrontational society than ever before, fighting still is not the answer to a problem. Actively seeking and making peace is. It's not as easy as fighting, but it is a lot less painful.

No matter what the other fellow does on the field, don't let him lure you into a fight. Uphold your dignity.
—COACH FRANK THOMAS

≫ **Making peace instead of fighting takes courage and strength, but it's certainly the less painful—and wiser—option.**

Big Red Elephants

Read Psalm 139:1–18.

"It was you who formed my inward parts; you knit me together in my mother's womb. I praise you, for I am fearfully and wonderfully made" (vv. 13–14).

The year 1930 is legendary in Alabama football history. In Coach Wallace Wade's final season, the Crimson Tide went 10–0, thrashed Washington State 24–0 in the Rose Bowl, and won the school's second national championship.

But all that's not really why 1930 holds such a special place in Alabama gridiron history. It was the season the school got its mascot: the elephant.

"The Elephant Story" tells the tale. On October 4, in the second game of the season, Alabama crushed Ole Miss 64–0. In a story on the game, sportswriter Everett Strupper of the *Atlanta Journal* wrote, "At the end of the [first] quarter, the earth started to tremble, there was a distant rumble that continued to grow. Some excited fans in the stands bellowed, 'Hold your horses, the elephants are coming.'"

Why would the Alabama faithful say such a thing? Because Wade had the unusual strategy that season of starting his second team. So when the second quarter started, "out stomped the Alabama varsity." Strupper wrote, "It was the first time that I had seen [the starters], and the size of the entire eleven nearly knocked me cold."

Strupper and other writers that season took to referring to Alabama as the "Red Elephants." The name stuck, and today Big Al lives.

Admit it: You go along with the kids' trip to the zoo because you think it's a cool place, too. And Big Al doesn't really look much like the elephants you see in a zoo, does he?

All that variety of life on display is mind-boggling. Who could conceive of an elephant, a walrus, or a prairie dog? But who could conceive of you? You are one of a kind, unique, a creative masterpiece that will never be duplicated. God's behind it all.

If you had a manufacturer's label, it might say, "Lovingly handmade in heaven by #1—God."

> *I really dig Hannibal. Hannibal had real guts.*
> *He rode elephants into Cartilage.*
> —MIKE TYSON

▷ **You may consider some painting a work of art, but the real masterpiece is you.**

A Strategy for Success

Read Joshua 6:1–20.

"You shall march around the city . . . for six days. . . . On the seventh day you shall march around the city seven times, the priests blowing the trumpets. . . . Then all the people shall shout with a great shout; and the wall of the city will fall down" (vv. 3–5).

Johnny Dee was a master of mind games and basketball games. He coached Alabama to a 68–25 record and an SEC championship from 1953 to 1956. He may have pulled his greatest motivational stunt against Georgia Tech in 1955—when he refused to go back onto the court with his team.

Tech led at halftime, and Leon Marlaire recalled to Clyde Bolton in *The Basketball Tide* what happened in the dressing room. Dee announced to a stunned team that he wasn't going back out for the second half.

When the refs gave a time warning, Dee was nowhere around. All-American George Linn said, "Hey, we'd better do something. He's not coming out." So the bewildered players wandered back onto the court. Marlaire said, "We were standing out on the court wondering what to do without a coach.

Linn said, 'Well, let's start the same group that started the game. You know he would do that.'"

So they played—and took the lead in the fourth quarter. Marlaire said Dee had been peeking out the dressing-room door, and suddenly "he came running up to our bench and called time out. . . . He yelled, 'That's what I want! That's my team!'"

The Tide won the game 76–72.

Successful living takes strategic planning of a kind more deliberate and long-range than Dee's unusual strategy against Tech. You go to school to improve your chances for a better job. You use plans to build your home. You plan for retirement. You deliberately map out your vacation. You even plan your children—sometimes.

Successful death takes planning, too, but God has taken care of that for us, devising the ultimate plan in Jesus Christ. Our best-laid plans may get wrecked by the economy or unexpected illness, but God's plan for eternity is foolproof. Jesus will not fail us.

> *If you don't know where you are going, you will wind up somewhere else.*
> —YOGI BERRA

> **Success in life takes planning and strategy; success in death does, too, and God has the plan for you.**

No Turning Back

Read Matthew 8:18–22.

"Jesus said to him, 'Follow me, and let the dead bury their own dead'" (v. 22).

In 1958 a new day dawned at the University of Alabama. Bear Bryant came back home.

While excitement and anticipation were rampant among the Tide faithful, the players on campus were also apprehensive. They knew the stories of the Junction Boys at Texas A&M. In *Crimson Nation,* Eli Gold described Bear Bryant's now-legendary football boot camp as "taking a team off-campus during a ninety-five-degree Texas summer, clearing a rocky dirt field, and setting them to doing intense two-a-days and at the end of the day having them crash in a non-air-conditioned dorm."

Bryant quickly made his intentions clear to his new players. "I came here to make Alabama a winner again," he told them in an early meeting. And what did he expect from them? "If you're not committed to winning ball games, to making your grades, go ahead and get your stuff and move out of the dorm," Bryant barked. "Pull out so we can concentrate on the players who want to play."

Twenty-two players did pull out that first spring, and six-teen more followed in the fall. The ones who stayed were committed to winning football at Alabama.

When you realize you've committed to something and there's no turning back, a combination of excitement and fear twists your gut into knots. Maybe it was the first time you went to camp and watched your parents drive away. The day you became a soldier. Your wedding day.

Commitment is often considered a dirty word in our society these days, a synonym for *chains*, an antonym for *freedom*. Perhaps that's why many people consider Jesus so scary—because he demands commitment.

But *commitment* actually means purpose and meaning, especially when you're talking about your life. Commitment makes life worthwhile.

Just ask those players who stuck it out when the Bear came. Four years after he arrived, they were national champions.

The quality of a person's life is in direct proportion
to his commitment to excellence, regardless of his chosen
field of endeavor.
—VINCE LOMBARDI

▶ **Rather than constraining you, commitment lends**
meaning to your life, releasing you to pursue your life's
purpose.

Young Blood

Read: Jeremiah 1:4–10.

"Do not say, 'I am only a boy'; . . . for I am with you to deliver you, says the LORD" (vv. 7a, 8).

No matter how legendary your reputation is, when you're a freshman on the Alabama gymnastics team, you start slowly. After all, this is one of the nation's powerhouse programs, so you have to work your way into the lineup.

Yeah, right. Tell that to Terin Humphrey.

Her reputation preceded her because Humphrey came to the Capstone in the winter of 2005 as one of the most celebrated freshmen in history, the sport's first Olympian. She won two silver medals in the 2004 Athens games and was also a member of the gold medal–winning American team at the 2003 World Championships. Her pressure-packed floor routine was pivotal to the Americans' triumph.

Still, this was collegiate gymnastics at the highest level. As Matt Scalici said in the *Crimson White* article "Humphrey Taking Alabama by Storm," "Humphrey was expected to have a somewhat slower start" after she spent the fall of 2004 on tour.

But according to Scalici, "Her start was anything but slow, climbing to fourth in the nation on the uneven bars and gaining a No. 1 ranking on the balance beam by the second week of the regular season." In her third meet she added another event, the vault, and promptly tied for first.

So much for the transition to the elite level of competition in the SEC.

Life usually requires that you spend time on the bench as a reserve, waiting your chance to play with the big boys and girls. You probably rode some pine in high school. You started college as a lowly freshman. You began work at an entry-level position.

Paying your dues is traditional, but that shouldn't stop you from doing something bold right away, as Terin Humphrey did. Too young, too inexperienced—they're just excuses. God certainly doesn't pay any attention to them in issuing a call. After all, the younger you are, the more time you have to serve.

You're only young once, but you can be immature forever.
—FORMER MAJOR LEAGUER LARRY ANDERSEN

≫ **Youth is no excuse for not serving God; it just gives you more time.**

A Matter of Perspective

Read John 20:11–18.

"Mary stood weeping outside the tomb" (v. 11).

The weather was awful.

Careful eyes watched the skies for tornadoes. As Evan Woodbery described the weather for the *Crimson White,* "There was consistent rain. Sometimes it came in a mist, sometimes in a deluge." And it got colder as the evening wore on.

So what were most of the thirty thousand–plus folks doing out in that weather?

Having a good time.

"We came because of the weather," said Brandon Brown, who wasn't going to let a little storm stop him from cheering for the Tide—or from painting his chest in hopes of getting on television. "I'll be here until [Tide quarterback] Andrew Zow gives me a ride home," said Andrew Wilson, who didn't let a little miserable weather keep him from whooping it up at the first Alabama game he had ever attended.

And they had quite a bit to cheer about. In that frightful weather of November 29, 2001, at Legion Field, the Tide defeated Southern Mississippi 28–15. That made the weather a whole lot nicer—at least on the Alabama sidelines. Over on the Southern Miss side, things were wet and miserable. The visitors shivered and were generally gloomy, but the Tide fans frolicked, hollered, and generally had a rollicking good time.

It was all a matter of perspective.

Three of life's truths: If it feels good or tastes good, it's probably bad for you; lettuce is really clumpy grass; and everyone will die. That last one is tougher to swallow than lettuce. (See truth number two.) You can't avoid death, but you can determine how you perceive it before it comes calling.

Is it fearful, dark, and fraught with peril and uncertainty? Or is it a passageway to glory, the Light, and loved ones—an elevator ride to paradise?

It's a matter of perspective that depends on whether you're standing by Jesus's side.

For some people it's the end of the rainbow,
but for us it is the end of the finish line.
—Rower Larisa Healy

> **Whether death is your worst enemy or a solicitous chauffeur is a matter of perspective; where do you stand?**

Decisions, Decisions

Read Judges 16:4–21.

"Finally, after she had nagged him with her words day after day, and pestered him, he was tired to death. So he told her his whole secret" (vv. 16–17).

One of Alabama's greatest football players ever wound up in Tuscaloosa because of a lousy train schedule.

In Richard Scott's *Legends of Alabama Football,* Hank Crisp, longtime Alabama assistant coach and athletic director, called Allison Thomas Stanislaus "Pooley" Hubert "the greatest player I ever coached in over forty years." Hubert was Alabama's second all-American and, as Scott said, "one of the primary reasons why Alabama emerged as a national college football power in the 1920s."

He left home to play football for Princeton only to arrive too late to take the entrance exams. So he headed south to Virginia but didn't like it there. Then he went on down to Atlanta and Georgia Tech but "was too late, and they didn't let freshmen play."

A Tech coach suggested Hubert give the University of Georgia a try, which sounded fine since the twenty-year-old freshman just wanted to play football somewhere. Then came one of those strange, unexpected twists of fate that change a school's football fortune, perhaps forever.

Hubert asked the train-station clerk "if the Southern Railway went to Athens, and he said no. So I asked him what was the next school on the Southern, and he said Alabama." Hubert bought a ticket, and thus did "Pooley" show up in Tuscaloosa.

Perhaps decisions made for frivolous reasons have determined how your life unfolds. You had that first date with your spouse because you wanted a free meal. You changed majors in college because the teacher in one required course demanded too much reading. Some of those spur-of-the-moment decisions may have turned out better than carefully considered ones (others, not so good—see the story of Samson).

The most important decision of your life is what to do with Jesus. Carefully considered or spontaneous—how you get to Jesus doesn't matter; all that matters is that you get there.

If you make a decision that you think is the proper one at the time, then that's the correct decision.
—Basketball coach John Wooden

▶ **A decision for Jesus may be spontaneous or considered; what counts is that you make it.**

Beyond the Games

Read Galatians 5:16–26.

"Live by the Spirit, I say, and do not gratify the desires of the flesh. . . . Those who do such things will not inherit the kingdom of God" (vv. 16, 21).

Some of Alabama's greatest athletic success stories have little to do with the games themselves.

For instance, only the most diehard Crimson Tide basketball fan would readily recall Lucky Williams, a guard who completed his career in 2005. He never started a game, played in fewer than thirty games, and averaged fewer than three minutes a game when he did play. On the basis of the stat sheet, Williams was not a success.

But cold facts don't tell the whole story. Williams is a native of Nigeria who learned to play basketball barefoot, on dirt courts. When he came to America, he liked what he saw of his new home. America "looked like a nice place and a place where you want to come—a place with opportunities," he told Buddy Hughes of the *Crimson White*.

Williams made the most of his time at Alabama, graduating with a degree in management. He also left behind a rare legacy: Folks loved him. He was such a favorite of the students that they consistently urged Coach Mark Gottfried to put him in. Anyone who talked about Williams said he was a "good guy" and a "nice" person. Coach Gottfried told Hughes, "I'd like to adopt him one day. He's such a great person."

Are you a successful person? How do you define success? Is it based on your investments, the square footage of your house, that title on your office door?

Certainly the world determines success by wealth, fame, prestige, awards, and toys. Our culture screams that life is all about gratifying your own needs and wants. If it feels good, do it.

A better way to approach success is through the spiritual rather than the physical realm. The goal is not money or back-slaps by sycophants but eternal life spent with God. Success of that kind is forever.

Success demands singleness of purpose.
—VINCE LOMBARDI

> **Success isn't permanent, and failure isn't fatal— unless you're talking about your relationship with God.**

The Beautiful People

Read Matthew 23:23–28.

"Woe to you, scribes and Pharisees, hypocrites! For you are like whitewashed tombs, which on the outside look beautiful, but inside they are full of the bones of the dead and of all kinds of filth" (v. 27).

Never underestimate the power of a woman whose beauty is more than skin deep.

In Bart Starr's case, the combination of one woman's beautiful face and beautiful character led him to a pair of decisions that determined the course of his life—and made football history.

In the summer of 1951 Starr was headed to Kentucky to play quarterback. But, Starr told Richard Scott in *Legends of Alabama Football*, "I had started dating a beautiful young lady in high school, and I think God gave me enough common sense to realize that if I went to the University of Kentucky in Lexington and she stayed in Alabama and went to Auburn University that I would lose her."

So that "beautiful young lady" led Starr to opt for Alabama "so I could chase her during the off season." Bart and Cherry were married after his sophomore year.

Starr's career at Alabama ended in disappointment. His senior year he rode the bench for an 0–10 team as a new head coach opted for a run-oriented quarterback, which Starr wasn't.

But remember that beautiful young woman who was more than just a pretty face? She wouldn't let Starr give up on his dream. She supported him as he struggled to land a spot with the Green Bay Packers. The rest is NFL legend.

Remember the brunette who sat behind you in history class? Or was it the blonde in English? Or that hunk from the next apartment who washes his car every Saturday morning, forcing you to find some excuse to get outside?

We do love those beautiful people.

Jesus never urged folks to walk around with body odor and unwashed hair. He did, however, admonish us to avoid being overly concerned with physical beauty, which fades with age despite tucks and Botox. Inner beauty, which reveals itself in the practice of justice, mercy, and faith, is not only lifelong— it's eternal.

> *Ah, the glories of women's sports: the camaraderie.*
> *The quiet dignity. The proud refusal to buy into traditional*
> *stereotypes of beauty.*
> —SPORTS ILLUSTRATED FOR WOMEN

≫ **When it comes to looking good, it's what's inside that counts.**

Bad Times—Good Witness

Read Philippians 1:3–14.

"What has happened to me has actually helped to spread the gospel, . . . and most of the brothers and sisters, having been made confident in the Lord by my imprisonment, dare to speak the word with greater boldness and without fear" (vv. 12, 14).

He "rose to the status of cultural icon." He "can be mentioned alongside names such as Babe Ruth [and] Joe DiMaggio," wrote David Scott in *Legends of Alabama Football*. "He" is Joe Willie Namath.

From 1962 to 1964 Namath set Crimson Tide records for completions and passing yards. He was the first quarterback in pro-football history to pass for more than four thousand yards in a season. He became the biggest sports star in America when he guaranteed a Jets victory in Super Bowl III—and delivered, effecting a merger of the two pro-football leagues and permanently changing the landscape of American sports.

Those were good times. But, Namath told Scott, "I remember Coach Bryant telling us when we were freshmen that we'd probably remember the bad times more than the good, the bad games and the losses more than the good games and the wins—and he was right."

Namath was suspended his junior year at Alabama and missed the Sugar Bowl. In his early years with the Jets, the team lost and he threw more interceptions than touchdowns. The press wrote of his fondness for New York's nightlife and women. His knees deteriorated, taking some of that awesome talent with them. Even for one of Alabama's greatest sports legends, bad times were part of the mix.

Loved ones die. You're downsized. Your biopsy looks cancerous. Your spouse could be having an affair. Hard, tragic times are as much a part of life as breath. How will you handle them? You can buckle to your knees in despair and cry, "Why me?" Or you can fall to your knees in prayer and ask, "What do I do with this?"

Setbacks and tragedies are opportunities to reveal and to develop true character and abiding faith. Your faithfulness—not your skipping merrily along through life without pain—is what reveals the depth of your love for God.

> *If I were to say, "God, why me?" about the bad things, then I should have said, "God, why me?" about the good things that happened in my life.*
> —ARTHUR ASHE

▷ **Faithfulness to God requires faith even in—especially in—the hard times.**

The Eye of a Needle

Read Matthew 19:23–26.

"Again I tell you, it is easier for a camel to go through the eye of a needle than for someone who is rich to enter the kingdom of God" (v. 24).

The fans voted it the most important play in the history of Legion Field: Van Tiffin's fifty-two-yard field goal that beat Auburn 25–23 on November 30, 1985.

Eli Gold wrote in *Crimson Nation,* "It was an astounding, pressure-packed, and very long kick." For Tiffin the kick was a dream—sort of. "As a kicker, you want the opportunity to make a last-second field goal," he said. "That's a dream any kicker would have. But you don't want it to be fifty-two yards!"

Tiffin told Gold he didn't think he'd be going in. "There were two drunk guys in the stadium hollering, 'Hey! It's gonna all come down to you!' But I didn't worry about it because it wasn't looking too good."

It sure wasn't. Auburn went ahead 23–22 with less than a minute left, but quarterback Mike Shula led the Tide into position for Tiffin's momentous kick. Shula hit receiver Greg Richardson over the middle, and Richardson dragged an Auburn defender out of bounds to stop the clock with only seven seconds left.

Considering the distance and the circumstances, those goal posts must have looked about as wide as the eye of a needle to "Ol' Thunderfoot," as Tiffin became known. But Tiffin nailed the kick for the win.

Are you rich? Even if you're struggling to keep the bills current and putting off buying that fishing boat, the answer is probably yes. Compared with much of the world, most Americans are wealthy.

So was Jesus saying that because you've got a few dollars in the bank the doors of heaven will slam in your face? No, but he was serving notice that you must do something that, for many, is as difficult as pushing a camel through the eye of a needle: In God alone, not in the riches and luxuries of this world, you must trust.

To be able to give away riches is mandatory if you wish to possess them. This is the only way that you will be truly rich.
—MUHAMMAD ALI

⫸ **Be sure you don't allow any riches or luxuries to come before God in your life.**

Ten to Remember

Read Exodus 20:1–17.

"Then God spoke all these words: 'I am the LORD your God . . . ; you shall have no other gods before me'"
(vv. 1–3).

Not surprisingly, considering its success, the University of Alabama has had some real runaways in its long and storied football history.

The greatest Crimson Tide slaughter of all time occurred in 1922 when Alabama blasted Marion Institute 110–0. Apparently Marion had had enough, for that was the last time the two teams met, ending a series that had begun in 1902 with an 81–0 Alabama victory. Bama had a 9–0 edge in the series and outscored Marion in the process 482–0.

That 110–0 win is the only time Alabama has broken the century mark, though the 1921 team came close with a 95–0 blasting of Bryson (Tennessee).

The remainder of the top-ten Alabama wins in order of margin of victory are an 89–0 romp over Delta State in 1951; an 81–0 runaway against Birmingham-Southern in 1913 and that 81–0 blasting of Marion Institute in 1902; a 1916 80–0 pasting of Birmingham-Southern; a 71–0 shellacking of Vanderbilt in 1945; a 77–6 walloping of Virginia Tech in 1973; a 74–7 laugher against Clemson in 1931; and 1915's 67–0 win over Birmingham-Southern. (Coming in close are a pair of 66–0 wins, against Richmond in 1961 and California in 1973.)

For Alabama fans, this is a list to remember.

Today you've got your list, and you're ready to go: a gallon of paint and a water hose from the hardware store; dip, chips, peanuts, and sodas from the grocery store for tonight's neighborhood meeting; the dry cleaning; tickets for the high-school band concert; burgers and fries for lunch. Your list helps you remember.

God once made a list of things he wanted you to remember: the Ten Commandments. Just as your list reminds you to do something, so God's list reminds you how you're to act in your dealings with other people—and with him.

Society today treats the Ten Commandments as if they were the ten suggestions. Never compromise on right or wrong.
—COLLEGE BASEBALL COACH GORDIE GILLESPIE

> **God's top-ten list is a set of instructions on how you should conduct yourself with other people and with him.**

Name Dropping

Read Exodus 3:1–15.

"This is my name forever, and this my title for all generations" (v. 15).

As so much at Alabama does, a list of Crimson Tide nicknames begins with "The Bear."

Of course, there's "Broadway" Joe Namath and Kenny "The Snake" Stabler. And who could forget "The Dothan Antelope," Johnny Mack Brown, one of the Tide's greatest football players and certainly the university's most famous cowboy?

From David "Deuce" Palmer to Millard "Dixie" Howell (dubbed "The Human Howitzer" by legendary sportswriter Grantland Rice), Alabama's history is full of players with colorful nicknames. According to Clyde Bolton in *The Basketball Tide,* the roster of Alabama's first basketball players in 1913 included Old Grif, Burr, Pep, Dink, Lengthy, Amo, Mack, and Bunch.

Is not the most perfect nickname in all of Alabama lore Ozzie Newsome's "The Wizard of Oz"? Would Allison Thomas Stanislaus Hubert have been an all-American if he had not been known as "Pooley"? And wasn't the real "Italian Stallion" Johnny Musso and not Rocky Balboa?

Could they be anything but the "Crimson Tide"? But Eli Gold said in *Crimson Nation* it was not until the 1907 Auburn game, during Alabama's fifteenth season, that sportswriter Hugh Roberts of the *Birmingham Age-Herald* wrote, "The Alabama playes rolled over their opponents like a Crimson Tide."

These and other monikers are more than just imaginative nicknames slapped haphazardly upon Alabama players and coaches. They reflect widely held perceptions about the people named.

Nicknames and proper names do that. Try this list: Adolf Hitler, Pol Pot, Al Capone. Then try Mother Teresa, Jesus Christ, Mahatma Gandhi. Any doubt about which list you'd want your name associated with?

What does your name say about you? Honest, trustworthy, a seeker of the truth and a person of God? Or does the mention of your name cause your coworkers to whisper snide remarks, your neighbors to roll their eyes, or your friends to start making allowances for you?

Most important, what does your name say about you to God? He, too, knows you by name.

For when that One Great Scorer comes to mark against your name, He writes—not that you won or lost—but how you played the game.

—SPORTSWRITER GRANTLAND RICE

▷ **Live so that your name evokes positive associations by people you know, the public, and God.**

Small Seeds

Read Mark 4:30–32.

"[The kingdom of God] is like a mustard seed, which, when sown upon the ground, is the smallest of all the seeds on earth; yet when it is sown it grows up and becomes the greatest of all shrubs" (vv. 31–32).

Intercollegiate basketball came late to the University of Alabama.

As Clyde Bolton noted in *The Basketball Tide,* intercollegiate football started at Alabama in 1892; baseball was even older. Basketball did not arrive until 1913, and then primarily because of the efforts of D. V. Graves. He came to Alabama in 1911 as the coach of athletics, which meant he coached everything. He had played college basketball at Missouri, so he set about building a team.

The student newspaper noted that Alabama was "the only school of consequence in Dixie to neglect this rapidly growing branch of college athletics." The paper admitted, however, that this inaugural team was "more in the nature of an experiment to see if the interest in it will be sufficient to justify the athletic authorities in continuing the sport."

The first game was played at the Tuscaloosa YMCA against the Bessemer Athletic Club. Alabama lost in overtime 22–20, but basketball was here to stay.

Still, the crowd at that game was not as large as the ones that gather in the two-acre complex that is Coleman Coliseum today to watch the Crimson Tide play. Decades later D. V. Graves and those pioneer players would barely recognize the game they launched and would surely be surprised and delighted at how Alabama's basketball program has grown.

Most worthwhile aspects of life take time and tending to grow from small beginnings into something magnificent. A good marriage is that way. Your beautiful lawn didn't just appear. And children don't get to be responsible and caring adults overnight.

Your faith, too, must be nurtured over time. Remember those older folks you revered as saints when you were growing up? Such distinction is achieved, not awarded.

In life and in faith, it's okay to start small. Faith is a journey, not a destination. You'll keep growing, always moving on to bigger and better things in God.

Everybody is looking for instant success, but it doesn't work that way. You build a successful life one day at a time.
—LOU HOLTZ

▷ **Faith is a lifelong journey of growth.**

Debt Free

Read Colossians 2:8–15.

"God made you alive together with him, when he forgave us all our trespasses, erasing the record that stood against us with its legal demands. He set this aside, nailing it to the cross" (vv. 13–14).

Never let it be said the Alabama football program doesn't pay its debts—even when it takes thirty years to do it.

Clyde Bolton wrote in *The Crimson Tide* that football at Alabama "in the Gay Nineties was haphazard, to say the least." Alabama went through nine coaches its first fourteen seasons, as finding men who were knowledgeable about this new game was difficult.

The third Alabama head coach was Otto Wagonhurst, a University of Pennsylvania graduate who coached the 1896 season. His team went 2–1 with wins over the Birmingham Athletic Club and Mississippi State, sandwiched around a loss to Sewanee.

Back in those early days, the senior class sponsored the football team. Wagonhurst had accepted the job at a salary of $750, but the seniors could scrape together only $250 during the season. They put on a show in the spring, but it netted only $50, which they promptly sent to Wagonhurst.

Time passed until about thirty years later, after Alabama had become a football powerhouse, when the Athletic Association decided to make good on its debt to one of the Tide's pioneer coaches. According to Bolton, they located Wagonhurst, who was working for a rubber company in Akron, Ohio. He "was shocked to receive the remainder of his salary for coaching the 1896 team."

Debt is a way of life for many. Perhaps you finance your house, your car, your kids' college education, maybe even the furniture you sit on. You put incidental expenses on your credit cards, like that cruise to the Bahamas or your Alabama season football tickets. Your life is a ledger in which you work to make sure assets exceed liabilities.

But have you ever considered that you owe God for your life and everything in it? How in the world can you possibly repay such a massive debt? By giving that life back to him through faith in Jesus.

I won't give luck the credit. I give the credit to God.
—FORMER TENNESSEE QUARTERBACK TEE MARTIN

You are deeply in debt to God for everything you have, but what he wants as payback is simply your faith.

Tough Love

Read Mark 10:17–22.

"Jesus, looking at him, loved him and said, 'You lack one thing; go, sell what you own, and give the money to the poor, and you will have treasure in heaven; then come, follow me.' When he heard this, he was shocked and went away grieving" (vv. 21–22).

At a practice in 1980, according to Chris Warner in *SEC Sports Quotes*, Bear Bryant gathered his players around a man who was a stranger to most of them and said, "Boys, I'd like to introduce you to Coach Wallace Wade. He's the man responsible for the great tradition of Alabama football."

Wade coached Alabama from 1923 to 1930, and his teams put Alabama football on the national map. His record was 61–13–3, which included Alabama's first three national championships.

Wade's approach was one of tough love. As Clyde Bolton put it in *The Crimson Tide,* "Wade's players feared him." After he left Alabama for Duke, Wade was driving some players to a game. He stopped at an intersection but was dangerously close to a ditch. Bolton said, "The players tried to persuade each other to tell him, but none dared. When he attempted to drive away, the car turned over on its side, and they had to hitchhike to the game."

In Eli Gold's *Crimson Nation,* Bill Baty, who played his senior season for Wade at Alabama, said of his tough coach, "Wade was a disciplinarian of the first order. He coached a lot through fear rather than through warmth or persuasion." But Baty added that Wade's measures were effective and were appreciated by the players, including himself.

Strict with your kids? Expect them to abide by your rules? The immediate reward you receive may be an intense and loud "I hate you," a flounce, and a slammed door. So why do it? Because you're the parent; you love your children, and you want them to become responsible adults. It's tough love.

Jesus is tough on the ones he loves, too. That includes you. He expects you to do what he said—to do right. And a well-executed flounce won't change things. But hang tough; you'll be better for it—and thankful for it—in the end.

Never leave the field with a boy feeling you're mad at him. You can chew him out, but then pat him on the shoulder.
—LEGENDARY FLORIDA A&M COACH JAKE GAITHER

Jesus expects you to do what he has told you to do— but it's because he loves you and wants the best for you.

DAY 52

Dream World

Read Joel 2:26–28.

"Your old men shall dream dreams, and your young men shall see visions" (v. 28).

Dreams can come true. Sometimes it just takes a while.

For instance, Stephany Smith needed sixteen years to land her dream job.

Smith applied to become the head women's basketball coach at Alabama in 1989 after a stellar college career and one year as a graduate assistant at Harding University. "The Alabama job was the very first job I applied for," she told the *Crimson White*'s Richard D. Lee in "Bama Hires Smith." "I was just out of college and naïve enough to think I could go anywhere I wanted."

Unfortunately for Smith, the field of applicants included Rick Moody. He got the job and proceeded to become Alabama's all-time winningest coach, with a 311–176 record. Smith went on to gain experience as an assistant coach before she rolled up a 153–88 record in eight seasons as the head coach at Middle Tennessee State.

When Moody announced his retirement on February 21,

2005, Smith was listening. This time she had more than a dream and naïveté going for her: She had a track record as the coach of a team that played hard, aggressive basketball and usually wound up in the postseason.

So in April 2005—sixteen years after she originally applied—Smith got her dream job when athletics director Mal Moore introduced her as Alabama's new head coach.

Stephany Smith held on to her dream over the years, but have you? Remember that million dollars you were going to make before you were thirty? That perfect romance and ideal marriage? How about the great American novel you were going to write? Reality—not dreams—has come to demand your time, attention, and effort.

Besides, you understand that achieving your dreams requires a combination of persistence, timing, and providence. Making dreams come true is usually a long shot—unless your dreams are based on the promises of God. In that case, they're a sure thing.

An athlete cannot run with money in his pocket. He must run with hope in his heart and dreams in his head.
—OLYMPIC GOLD MEDALIST EMIL ZATOPEK

▶ **Dreams based on the world's promises are often crushed; those based on God's promises are a sure thing.**

A Frustrating Season

Read Exodus 32:1–20.

"Moses' anger burned hot, and he threw the tablets from his hands and broke them at the foot of the mountain"
(v. 19).

How can one of the greatest seasons in Alabama football history be frustrating?

In 1966 the Crimson Tide went 10–0 in the regular season. The only close game that year was an 11–10 win over Tennessee in which quarterback Ken Stabler rallied the Tide from ten down in the fourth quarter. Alabama then blasted Nebraska 34–7 in the Sugar Bowl.

So what happened that was frustrating?

As Richard Scott explained in *Legends of Alabama Football,* "Despite a perfect record and two previous national championships in 1964 and 1965, the Crimson Tide finished third in the polls." Regional prejudice clearly played a part in costing Alabama the national championship. Ranked ahead of them were Notre Dame and Michigan State, who that year deadlocked 10–10 when the Irish intentionally played for the tie late in the game. They both finished 9–0–1, but as Stabler noted, "Most of the votes came out of the East back then."

According to Stabler, "Coach Bryant went through the roof," but the great Bear could do nothing to change the results. So the team Bryant called the "greatest football team I've ever been associated with" endured what Scott says "was, and still is, one of the most disappointing and frustrating turn of events in the history of Alabama football."

The traffic light catches you when you're late for work or your doctor's appointment. The bureaucrat gives you red tape when you want help. Your child refuses to take schoolwork seriously. Makes your blood boil, doesn't it?

Frustration is part of God's testing ground that is life. What's important is not that you encounter frustration—that's a given—but how you handle it. Do you respond with curses, screams, and violence? Or a deep breath, a silent prayer, and calm persistence, even resolution when it's called for? Which way do you suppose God wishes you to respond?

> *A life of frustration is inevitable for any coach whose main enjoyment is winning.*
> —NFL HALL OF FAME COACH CHUCK NOLL

> **Frustration is a vexing part of life, but God expects us to handle it gracefully.**

From Student to Teacher

Read John 3:1–16.

"[Nicodemus] came to Jesus by night and said to him, 'Rabbi, we know that you are a teacher who has come from God'" (v. 2).

In forty-two years of coaching college basketball, none of Adolph Rupp's pupils had ever beaten him. Until C. M. Newton did it, that is.

Newton, who won 211 games from 1969 to 1980 as head coach of the Alabama men's basketball team, was a member of the 1951 Kentucky team that won the national championship. At Alabama he was 0–7 against his former teacher when he got his last shot at Rupp in 1972. The coaching legend had announced his retirement, effective at the end of the season.

Newton told Clyde Bolton in *The Basketball Tide* that what most impressed him about Rupp was his insistence on perfection. Rupp once said, "No team had ever played a perfect game, but someday he wanted one of his teams to." That meant no missed shots, no bad passes, no turnovers. Rupp also stressed the fundamentals of the game, teaching through instruction and repetition.

Alabama was still in the race for the SEC title, trailing Tennessee and Kentucky by one loss when the Wildcats came to Tuscaloosa in 1972. Alabama won 73–70 behind twenty points from Ray Odums. The Tide trailed by ten in the second half but rallied to grab what Newton called "the dangest win I've ever seen."

On this night, the pupil bested the teacher.

You can read this book, break ninety on the golf course, and be successful today at your job because somebody taught you. And as you learn, you become a teacher yourself. You teach your children how to play Monopoly and how to drive a car. You show rookies the ropes at the office and teach baseball's basics to the Little League team.

In all areas of your life, you learn from others and then you teach others. This includes your spiritual life. Somebody taught you about Jesus, and this, too, you must pass on.

The only reason we make good role models is because you guys look up to athletes. . . . The real role models should be your parents and teachers!
—NFL PLAYER DANTE HALL

> **In life, you learn and then you teach. This includes learning and teaching about Jesus, the most important lesson of all.**

A House Fit for a King

Read 2 Samuel 7:1–7.

"Go and tell my servant David: Thus says the LORD: . . . I have not lived in a house since the day I brought up the people of Israel from Egypt to this day, but I have been moving about in a tent and a tabernacle" (vv. 5–6).

Alabama's first football game was played in 1892, but it wasn't until 1929 that the team had a stadium to call home.

According to "Bryant-Denny Stadium: The History," through 1914 the Tide football team played at two sites on the Quad, one running parallel to Sixth Avenue, the second running parallel to University Boulevard. For the 1915 season the team moved to University Field, which was renamed Denny Field in 1920, a site two blocks east of the current stadium.

Even though it was an improvement, the new facility wasn't anything to get too excited about. Denny Field had only about eight thousand seats, all of them wooden bleachers.

From the beginning, though, Alabama had a home-field advantage no matter what kind of facilities the Tide used. Alabama's home record during those early years was a sparkling 87–11, including a remarkable 43–2 record on Denny Field that included thirty-five shutouts.

On October 5, 1929, though, a new age dawned for Alabama football with the dedication of Denny Stadium. (The Tide whipped Ole Miss 22–7 in the dedicatory game.) The state legislature renamed the facility Bryant-Denny Stadium in 1975, and a series of expansions from the original capacity of twelve thousand has created one of collegiate football's great sites, a jewel that seats more than ninety-two thousand people.

Stadium renovations occur because the home place can always be improved. You may feel your personal playing field could stand a little home improvement when you look into a mirror: too much weight, too little weight, hair the wrong color, too tall, too short. We tend to gauge our bodies against an impossible standard Hollywood and fashion magazines have created.

Someone must have liked your body, though, because someone created it. That someone is God, who personally fashioned your one-of-a-kind body and then gave it to you. Your body is a house fit for a king—the King.

If you don't do what's best for your body, you're the one who comes up on the short end.
—JULIUS ERVING

▷ **You may not have a fine opinion of your body, but God thought enough of it to personally create it for you.**

Unsolved Mysteries

Read Romans 11:25–36.

"O the depth of the riches and wisdom and knowledge of God! How unsearchable are his judgments and how inscrutable his ways!" (v. 33).

Bear Bryant was part of a mystery that went unsolved for fifty-two years.

In 1934 the Crimson Tide whipped Tennessee 13–6 on their way to an undefeated season and a Rose Bowl win over Stanford. During the game Bryant was ejected for throwing a punch that broke Tennessee fullback Phil Dickens's nose. The question for the ages has been whether Bryant actually did it.

In *Third Saturday in October* Al Browning cited sportswriter Zipp Newman: "The officials did Bryant a grave injustice. He was fifteen yards in back of the line of scrimmage." The papers reported that even the Tennessee players agreed the referees got the wrong man. Bryant, though, only halfheartedly denied he had slugged Dickens—perhaps because, as Browning said, he liked the spotlight.

So who broke Dickens's nose?

In 1986 Alabama tackle Bill Lee fessed up. He told Browning, "I did it. I'm the one the officials should have nabbed." At last the mystery was solved.

Or was it? Lee went on to claim it was all an accident. "I stumbled into Dickens as the play was ended. I fell on top of him and my elbow hit his nose. . . . An Alabama player would never do something like that to a Tennessee player, at least not intentionally."

Or would he?

Do you love a good whodunit or a rousing round of Clue? Do you match wits with TV detectives? A lot of folks like a good mystery. They like the challenge of uncovering what someone else wants to hide.

Some mysteries, though, are simply beyond our knowing. For instance, much about God remains mysterious. Why does he tolerate the existence of evil? What does he really look like? Why is he so fond of bugs?

We know for sure, though, that God is love, so we proceed with life, assured that one day all mysteries will be revealed.

If God wanted women to understand men, football would never have been created.
—Writer Roger Simon

> **God chooses to keep much about himself shrouded in mystery, but one day you will see and understand.**

DAY 57

No Getting Over It

Read Ephesians 2:1–10.

"By grace you have been saved through faith, and this is not your own doing; it is the gift of God" (v. 8).

Do you love Alabama football as much as Bill Baty did?

After he left Alabama, Baty played pro football for one year and then played two more years for George Washington University under an assumed name. He graduated from medical school, spent thirty years in the navy, and served as Alabama's team physician from 1959 until 1971.

But his playing days at Alabama were the stuff of his greatest dreams and his fondest memories. Baty played for Xen Scott and Wallace Wade from 1920 to 1923. When Alabama stunned heavily favored Pennsylvania 9–7 in 1922, in the biggest win in Tide football history to that point, Baty's twenty-five-yard run to the four-yard line set up Alabama's only touchdown. As Clyde Bolton wrote in *The Crimson Tide*, the win vindicated southern football and forever relegated to fairy tales the myth of the East's superiority.

In the early 1970s Baty spoke to Bolton about his love for Alabama football. He was almost seventy-one years old at the time and facing retirement. How much did his passion for Alabama still burn within him? He had lost a leg, but that would not keep him away from Tide games. "I'll be there as long as I can crawl," he said.

Once you experience Alabama football, you never get over it.

Some things in life have a way of getting under your skin and never letting go. Your passion may have begun the first time you rode in a convertible. Or when your breath was taken away the first time you saw the one who would become your spouse. Maybe you knew you were hooked the first time you walked into Bryant-Denny Stadium on game day. Or your world changed forever when you held your newborn child for the first time.

You can put God's love on that list, too. Once you encounter it, you'll never get over it.

You spend a good deal of your life gripping a baseball, and it turns out it was the other way around all the time.
—JIM BOUTON

> **Some things hit you so hard, you know you'll never be the same again; God's love is one of those things.**

DAY 58

Identity Crisis

Read Matthew 16:13–17.

"[Jesus] asked his disciples, 'Who do people say that the Son of Man is?' And they said, 'Some say John the Baptist, but others Elijah, and still others Jeremiah or one of the prophets'" (vv. 13–14).

Alabama's first basketball all-American was James "Lindy" Hood, who acquired his nickname because he once was mobbed by a crowd who thought he was Charles Lindbergh.

In 1927 Hood went out for football and went with the freshman, or "rat," team to New Orleans to play Tulane. After the team arrived at the stadium, Hood was sent back to the train station to pick up coach Hank Crisp's raincoat, since it looked like rain. As Clyde Bolton told it in *The Basketball Tide,* Hood found the streets packed with people expecting at any moment to see famed flyer Charles Lindbergh. "Hood had scarcely traversed a block when an urchin holloed, 'There goes Lindy.'" Hood turned to see the transatlantic flyer himself, but to his surprise the boy was pointing at him! "The crowd began to swarm around him. In vain he protested his true identity, and tried to get away. The crowd only milled more around him."

Finally Hood managed to escape by catching a streetcar headed for the Tulane campus. He was reluctant to tell the rest of the team about the incident, but he finally had to come clean about why he'd been gone for so long. From that day on he was "Lindy" to the Alabama students.

Who are you?

You may not be Spider-Man, but you do have a secret identity, don't you? It's hidden by the face you put on to meet the world each day, the expression that masks your secret longing to sail around the world. Maybe you hide how much you hate your job or how badly you wish your spouse would lose weight.

You are, in fact, more than what you appear. The world does not know your depth, but you shouldn't feel too bad about the shortsightedness of others. Many people still can't figure out who Jesus is.

> *Deep inside, we're still the boys of autumn, that magic time of the year that once swept us onto America's fields.*
> —ARCHIE MANNING

▶ **You are more than you appear to the world, but you're in good company; many don't know Jesus for who he is either.**

Confidence

Read Micah 7:5–7.

"As for me, I will look to the Lord, I will wait for the God of my salvation" (v. 7).

It was "perhaps the most famous play in Alabama football history," said Richard Scott in *Legends of Alabama Football*. And right before it, Tide tackle Marty Lyons told the opposing quarterback what he ought to do. Well, he was asked.

The Tide led Penn State 14–7 in the 1979 Sugar Bowl—the number-two team versus the number-one—when Penn State recovered a fumble at the Alabama nineteen with only 7:57 left in the game. The Nittany Lions moved to a first down at the Alabama eight. A run, a pass, a run—and they sat ten inches away from the Crimson Tide goal line. What now? Scott said Lyons and Penn State quarterback Chuck Fusina "found themselves standing near the ball and wondering what move the Penn State coaches would make next."

That's when Fusina looked over to Lyons and said, "What do you think?"

"Lyons, without blinking, simply replied, 'You should throw the ball.'"

But Penn State ran the ball—unsuccessfully—and the Tide won another national championship.

How could Lyons be so brash and cocky? He wasn't; Scott explained that "his words simply reflected the confidence of four years of working and preparing for moments such as these." As part of Bear Bryant's system, Lyons had total and complete confidence.

We all have confidence in many areas of life. You're confident the company you work for will pay you on time, or you wouldn't go to work. You turn the ignition confident your car will start. When you flip a switch, you expect the light to come on.

Our confidence in other people and in things is often misplaced, though. Companies go broke; the car battery dies; light bulbs burn out.

So where can you place your confidence with a certainty you won't be disappointed? In God. He will not fail you; he will never let you down.

> *When it gets right down to the wood-chopping,*
> *the key to winning is confidence.*
> —DARRELL ROYAL

> **People, things, and organizations will let you down.**
> **Only God deserves our absolute trust and confidence.**

Limited-Time Offer

Read Psalm 103.

"As for mortals, their days are like grass; they flourish like a flower of the field; for the wind passes over it, and it is gone. . . . But the steadfast love of the LORD *is from ever-lasting to everlasting on those who fear him" (vv. 15–17).*

H e was one of Alabama's greatest, a unanimous all-American and winner of the Butkus Trophy as the nation's top linebacker. And at age thirty-three he was gone.

According to Richard Scott in *Legends of Alabama Football,* Coach John Guy said Derrick Thomas came to Alabama in 1985 with a specific goal: to get his footprints and handprints in the captains' walk of fame at Denny Chimes. As it turned out, he was too modest. Before he left the Capstone, Thomas had his prints and a career that would see him named to the university's Team of the Century. As a junior he broke Corne-lius Bennett's school record for sacks; then, as a senior, Thomas broke his own record.

Scott relates that in January 2000 Thomas was on his way to the Kansas City Airport for a pro playoff game when his ve-hicle flipped three times on an icy road. He suffered a broken neck and spinal cord damage. He was paralyzed from the chest down, and he probably would never walk again.

Then, on February 8, on the way to a therapy session, "Derrick turned to speak to his mother. . . . Seconds later, he was dead, due to heart failure."

If you haven't yet, you will meet sudden, unexpected death head-on in your life. A heart attack or an accident will probably take—or has already taken—someone you know or love who is "too young to die."

God frequently comes under attack at such times because the death doesn't "make sense." The problem is that no one can see the whole picture, as God does. But you can know for sure (1) that God is in control; (2) that life is a limited-time offer; and (3) that with every moment, your time is running out, too.

Derrick Thomas knew that, and he prepared for it. In 1997 he rededicated his life to Christ—so that he might live forever with his Lord.

> *Knowing Derrick gave his life to the Lord,*
> *I can stand here in peace.*
>
> —KANSAS CITY CHIEFS FULLBACK TONY RICHARDSON

> **God's offer of eternal life through Jesus is for a limited time only; it expires at your death. Don't wait till it's too late.**

Using Your Head

Read Job 28.

"Truly, the fear of the LORD, that is wisdom; and to depart from evil is understanding" (v. 28).

There's no such thing as a thinking ballplayer on the court."

So spoke Jack Kubiszyn, a guard from Buffalo, New York, who set a school record in 1957 with forty-seven points against Mississippi College and averaged 24.5 points per game that season, also a record.

Kubiszyn favored reaction over thinking. "You have to think ahead of time and put it into your head like a computer," he told Clyde Bolton in *The Basketball Tide.*

Sometimes, though, Kubiszyn did use his head—especially one night against Holy Cross and the great Tom Heinsohn. During the game, according to Kubiszyn, Heinsohn ran "right over me—but the official called the foul on me." Coach Johnny Dee rushed onto the court, straddled Kubiszyn, and shouted at the official, "Look what they did to my boy!"

Kubiszyn recalled, "He picks up my head and asks me again if I'm OK, and I say I am, and he drops my head on the floor and hollers, 'Look what they did to my boy!' and he asks me again if I'm OK, and I say I am, and he drops my head on the floor again." Kubiszyn said this kept going "on and on, my head bouncing on the floor like a basketball and Coach Dee hollering at the official."

You're a thinking person. When you talk about using your head, you're speaking as Jack Kubiszyn did with his pregame planning, not in the sense of his bizarre experience during the Holy Cross game. Logic and reason are part of your psyche. A coach's bad call frustrates you, and your children's inexplicable behavior flummoxes you. Why can't people just think things through?

Jesus doesn't tell you to check your brains when you walk into a church or open the Bible. With your head and your heart you encounter God, who is, after all, the true source of wisdom.

> Football is more mental than physical,
> no matter how it looks from the stands.
> —HALL OF FAME LINEBACKER RAY NITSCHKE

> **Since God is the source of all wisdom, it's only logical that you encounter him with your mind as well as your emotions.**

Crazy as a Fox

Read Luke 13:31–35.

"Some Pharisees came and said to him, 'Get away from here, for Herod wants to kill you.' He said to them, 'Go and tell that fox for me. . . . Today, tomorrow, and the next day I must be on my way'" (vv. 31–33).

I thought he was crazy."

According to Richard Scott in *Legends of Alabama Football*, that was tackle Billy Neighbors's less-than-flattering assessment of Bear Bryant after meeting with the new Alabama head coach for the first time in 1958. Neighbors was part of Bryant's first recruiting class, and he went on to become a member of the College Football Hall of Fame. As Scott said, Neighbors "is widely regarded as one of the two best blockers in Alabama history, along with [John] Hannah."

What was it Bryant said in that first meeting that led Neighbors to question his sanity? He vowed that the freshmen, Neighbors included, would "be undefeated and win the national championship before y'all leave here—if you'll do what I tell you to do." And then there was the fact that Bryant had already kicked Neighbors's older brother Sid off the team when he showed up three pounds overweight.

But as history revealed and Scott recorded, Bryant was "crazy as a fox." Those freshmen who sat in fear and perplexity that first day won the national championship in 1961, the first of Bryant's six crowns. Neighbors played both ways on that team and was named all-American.

What some see as crazy often is, instead, shrewd.

Like the time you went into business for yourself or when you decided to go back to school. Maybe it was when you bought that dilapidated house and fixed it up. Or even when you invested in something few others saw the potential in, like that swampland near Orlando.

You know a good thing when you see it. And because Jesus went to Jerusalem in defiance of all apparent reason and logic, since he knew death awaited him there, you know that the best offer you'll ever get is the one he provided by that death: eternal life.

Football is easy if you're crazy.
—Bo Jackson

>> **It's so good it sounds crazy—but it's not: Through faith in Jesus, you can have eternal life with God.**

Playing by the Rules

Read Luke 6:1–11.

"They were filled with fury and discussed with one another what they might do to Jesus" (v. 11).

An annual tennis tournament is named for her. She was one of the original members of the University of Alabama's Tennis Hall of Fame. Roberta Alison may well be the greatest women's tennis player the Crimson Tide has ever had. But she isn't listed among those who lettered in women's tennis—and it's no misprint. What's going on here?

Well, Roberta Alison did letter, three times—for the men's tennis team.

In 1963 the SEC voted to allow women to play on the men's teams. Alabama coach Jason Morton had seen Alison play, and he convinced her to play for the men's team. (Women's-team play did not begin at Alabama until 1975.) She was the first female in the university's history to receive an athletic scholarship.

At age nineteen Alison took on the establishment; her presence broke all the rules. Some opposing coaches forfeited matches rather than allow their players to be "insulted" by playing a woman. The pressure on her was immense and intense, but as noted in "Alabama Legend: Roberta Alison," she "carried the entire affair with class and with some of the best tennis performances of that time."

How good was she? Alison was an SEC quarterfinalist, and as a senior she played against the best other schools could throw at her. Her record was 9–6.

Society has unspoken but powerful rules in place about who and what is acceptable. Despite official sanction, Alison was harassed because she violated an unspoken rule of the time that said women don't play with the men.

Jesus also encountered societal rules that delineated the company he should keep. But he chose love instead of the rules and mingled freely with society's outcasts.

You, too, have to choose when you find yourself in the presence of someone whom society says is undesirable. Will you choose disdain or love? Are you willing to be a rebel for love—as Jesus was?

> *I believe in rules. Sure I do. If there weren't any rules,*
> *how could you break them?*
>
> —LEO DUROCHER

➤ **Society's rules dictate who is acceptable and who is not, but love in the name of Jesus knows no such distinctions.**

Top Secret

Read Romans 2:1–16.

"Their conflicting thoughts will accuse or perhaps excuse them on the day when, according to my gospel, God, through Jesus Christ, will judge the secret thoughts of all" (vv. 15–16).

Bear Bryant had a secret so big he was worried spies would try to discover it, so he practiced what Eli Gold, in *Crimson Nation,* called "complete subterfuge."

A tarp was hung around the practice field fence to discourage the curious. Most Tide practices were closed to the public and to the press. When Bryant did allow the public into practices, the players changed what they were practicing, then went back to the real exercises when the outsiders left.

What was Bryant's precious secret?

The wishbone offense. Three weeks before the 1971 season began, Bryant announced that Alabama was switching to the newfangled offense he had learned from Texas head coach Darrell Royal.

Only as the opening game neared against heavily favored Southern Cal was the secret told to the broadcast crew. They "were sworn to absolute secrecy—they were told not even to tell their families" or to alert the Trojan broadcast crew, which normally they would have done as a courtesy.

In Los Angeles on September 10, 1971, Bear Bryant unveiled his secret weapon. According to Gold, "The wishbone was a smash" as Alabama stunned the Trojans 17–10; the Crimson Tide was off to an undefeated season and the SEC championship.

Against all odds and all the prying eyes, Bear had kept his secret.

As Bear Bryant was about his wishbone offense, you have to be vigilant about your personal information. In our information age, a lot of data about you—from credit reports to what movies you rent—is readily available. People you don't know may know a lot about you—or at least they can find out. And some of them may use that information for harm.

That's why it's especially comforting to know that God, the one before whom you have no secrets, is not your enemy but is on your side.

I believe in God. He is the secret of my success.
—ALGERIAN OLYMPIAN NOUREDDINE MORCELI

> **We have no secrets before God; good thing he's on our side.**

The Knock on the Door

Read Revelation 3:20–21.

"Listen! I am standing at the door, knocking; if you hear my voice and open the door, I will come in to you" (v. 20).

Bear Bryant hated losing, but he also loathed tie games. He is generally credited with declaring, "A tie is like kissing your sister." He hated one particular tie so much that in his postgame anger he kicked down a locker-room door.

In 1965, a national championship year for the Tide, they won the SEC and outscored Nebraska 39–28 in the Orange Bowl; but the game against Tennessee finished in a 7–7 tie.

After the game, a frustrated Bryant and his equally frustrated team discovered that their dressing-room door was locked. The coach ordered an Alabama state trooper to shoot the door open. Junior tackle Jerry Duncan told Al Browning in *Third Saturday in October*, the surprised trooper replied, "Coach, I might kill three or four people if I do that." At that Bryant kicked the door down—"just took it off its hinges," Duncan said.

The racket drew the attention of a Birmingham Police Department officer, who rushed into the dressing room, saw the busted door, and was instantly angry over the destruction of university property. Browning described the scene:

"'Who knocked down that door?' the police officer said to Bryant.

"'I did,' Bryant said after yanking a cigarette from his mouth.

"'Well, OK, Coach Bryant,' the police officer said, before hurriedly exiting."

Everything's calm until someone knocks on your front door. The dog erupts into a barking frenzy. Your spouse calls, "Can you get that?" You tell the kids to answer the door, whereupon they whine in unison, "I'm busy."

So you leave the comfort of your favorite chair, pausing to peek through the curtains. A stranger, a friend, or a Girl Scout with cookies—it makes no difference. You open the door.

Today Jesus stands knocking at the door of your heart like a polite and unassuming guest. He won't kick in the door. He'll come in only if you invite him. But he's a visitor you don't want to miss.

Opportunity may knock, but you must open the door.
—Wrestling sportswriter and official Bill Welker

> *Jesus won't barge into your life; he will come in only when you open the door and invite him.*

When You Just Know

Read 2 Corinthians 5:6–10.

"We are always confident; even though we know that while we are at home in the body we are away from the LORD—for we walk by faith, not by sight" (vv. 6–7).

hit it well," Phillip Doyle said in Al Browning's *Third Saturday in October.*

"It" was a forty-seven-yard field-goal attempt on the last play of the 1990 game against Tennessee. When Doyle hit it, he knew it was good.

It had to be. Not a single touchdown was scored in a game that was a throwback to the football of decades ago. The teams were tied 3–3 after the first quarter before Doyle kicked a twenty-six-yarder in the third quarter and Tennessee answered with a fifty-one-yard field goal in the fourth quarter. That left the score tied at six.

With 1:35 remaining, Stacy Harrison blocked Tennessee's attempt to win with a fifty-yard field goal. He blocked the kick so hard that it rolled all the way to the Volunteers' thirty-seven. At that moment Harrison just knew the Tide would win. "I don't think anybody on our side thought Phillip Doyle would miss a field goal to win it," he said.

The Tide picked up seven yards, running the clock down to four seconds, and turned the game over to Doyle. Harrison and his teammates knew they would win the moment the blocked field goal rolled into Tennessee territory. Doyle knew they had won the moment toe met leather.

They just knew.

They knew in the same way you know certain things in your life. That your spouse loves you, for instance. That you're good at your job. That tea should be iced and sweetened. That a bad day fishing is still better than a good day at work.

You know that Bear Bryant was the greatest football coach ever and that the Crimson Tide is the only team worth pulling for. You know these things even though no mathematician or philosopher can prove any of this on paper.

It's the same way with faith in Jesus: You just know.

> *It's what you learn after you think you know it all that counts.*
>
> —EARL WEAVER

>> **A life of faith is lived in certainty and conviction: You just know you know.**

Can't Go Wrong

Read Galatians 6:7–10.

"Let us not grow weary in doing what is right, for we will reap at harvest time, if we do not give up" (v. 9).

Safiya Ingram had just won an SEC championship—and she gave it back.

Sixty-four meters was the mark for Ingram's hammer throw at the 2000 SEC Outdoor Track and Field Championships. That throw won her the SEC championship and set a new Alabama record. She automatically qualified for the NCAA championships.

But then, according to "Safiya Ingram: 2000 NCAA Sportsperson of the Year," Ingram "looked over at her coach Sandy Fowler with a question on her face," because she knew the mark was wrong. "She knew she had thrown well, but sixty-four meters seemed long."

Fowler said, "When she looked over at me with that look, I knew she had a question about the mark. I told her she could ask for a remeasurement, but it would have to come from her. I couldn't do it for her."

Call for a remeasurement because the mark was too long?

Unheard of. But that's what Ingram did. Sure enough, the correct distance was fifty-four meters. She finished second and lost the school record, but Safiya Ingram "had done what was right in her heart."

She not only made it to the NCAA championships and was named all-American in the discus, but the NCAA named her the 2000 NCAA Outstanding Sportsperson of the Year. Ingram was honored for displaying the highest ideals of sportsmanship.

Most important for her, she did the right thing.

Doing the right thing is easy when it's little stuff. Giving the quarter back when the cashier gives you too much change, helping a lost child at the mall, or putting the two dollars in the honor box at your favorite fishing hole.

But what about when it costs you? Every day you have chances to do the right thing, but does your decision depend upon your calculation of the odds of getting caught?

In the world's eyes, you can't go wrong doing wrong when you won't get caught.

In God's eyes, you can't go wrong doing right. Ever.

> *One person practicing sportsmanship is better than a hundred teaching it.*
> —KNUTE ROCKNE

> **As far as God is concerned, you can never go wrong doing right.**

Promises, Promises

Read 2 Corinthians 1:16–20.

"In [Jesus Christ] every one of God's promises is a 'Yes'" *(v. 20).*

on McNeal's football career began because he made a promise that he knew he wouldn't have to keep—yet he kept it anyway.

McNeal was one of the greatest of Alabama's players, an all-American cornerback in 1979 and a member of Alabama's Team of the Century who played ten years in the pros.

In *Legends of Alabama Football,* Richard Scott said a high-school coach saw McNeal in physical education class and asked him to try out for the football team. McNeal knew his dad wouldn't let him play because he was needed on the farm, but that was an excuse. "Really and truly, I didn't want to play," he said. But he promised the coach that if his dad okayed it, he would come out for the team.

To McNeal's surprise—and disappointment—his dad told him he could play if he could still manage his chores. He kept his word and went out for football as he had promised.

He had some problems: He was late for his first practice

because he couldn't figure out how to put on his ill-fitting uniform. And his ears bled until a coach discovered McNeal had thrown away his ear pads, thinking he didn't need them. The rest is history, though, all because Don McNeal kept a promise he'd made.

The promises you make don't say much about you; the promises you keep tell everything.

The promise to your daughter to be there for her softball game. To your son to help him with his math homework. To your parents to visit them soon. To your spouse to remain faithful until death parts you. To your neighbors to help them move. And remember what you promised God?

God operates on this simple premise: Promises made are promises kept. Those to whom you make promises expect the same from you—even when, like Don McNeal, you don't really want to.

In the everyday pressures of life, I have learned that God's promises are true.
—MAJOR LEAGUER GARRET ANDERSON

> **God keeps his promises, just as those who rely on you expect you to keep yours.**

A Joyful Noise

Read Psalm 100.

"Make a joyful noise to the LORD, all the earth" (v. 1).

If it's game day at the University of Alabama, it must be noisy.

The most noticeable and joyful noise of all comes when the Million Dollar Band cranks up. "Million Dollar Band: History and Facts" says the band began in 1913 as a fourteen-member unit under the direction of Gustav Wittig. The unit was led by students before eventually achieving national prominence under Colonel Carleton K. Butler in the 1930s.

In the early days the band didn't exactly have it easy. Money was always a problem. The 1948 Alabama football media guide noted that the band was really struggling in 1922 and could get to the Georgia Tech game only by asking downtown merchants for money. The students did such a good job of raising money that rather than riding in their customary day coach, which meant they sat up all night, they "finally got a tourist sleeper and put two to a lower and two to an upper berth." While these weren't the most luxurious accommodations, the band members thought they were just "swell."

According to the media guide, during the Tech game a sportswriter said to Alabama alumnus W. C. "Champ" Pickens, "You don't have much of a team; what do you have at Alabama?" Impressed by the band's fund-raising abilities, Pickens answered, "A Million Dollar Band." And thus a name was born.

Maybe you can't play a lick or carry a tune in the proverbial bucket. Or perhaps you do know your way around a guitar or a keyboard and can sing "Sweet Home Alabama" on karaoke night without causing the hounds to howl. But unless you're a professional musician, how well you play or sing really doesn't matter. What counts is that you have music in your heart, and sometimes you have to turn it loose.

The source of that music in your heart appreciates a little racket tossed his way, too. Send some joyful noise—praise—to God.

I like it because it plays old music.
—Pitcher Tug McGraw on his 1954 Buick

➤ **You call it music; others may call it noise. If it's joyful, send some God's way.**

DAY 70

Strange but True

Read 1 Corinthians 1:18–31.

"The message about the cross is foolishness to those who are perishing, but to us who are being saved it is the power of God" (v. 18).

The 1942 Cotton Bowl is certainly among the strangest games in Alabama history.

Under Coach Frank Thomas the Tide was 8–2 in 1941 with a squad about which Thomas said, "I've never seen as many great backs on one team." On the train ride to Dallas, according to Clyde Bolton in *The Crimson Tide,* Thomas said he saw "no way" the opponent, Texas A&M, could stop his backs.

But in that game the backs weren't the deciding factor at all.

Consider the following statistics: Alabama made one first down; Texas A&M had thirteen. Bama had seventy-five yards total offense; the Aggies rolled up 309 yards. The Tide completed one pass; A&M completed thirteen. Alabama ran thirty-two plays the entire game; Texas A&M had seventy-nine snaps.

And yet Alabama won the game 29–21, and it wasn't really that close.

How in the world?

Here's the statistic that makes those others meaningless: twelve Texas A&M turnovers. Alabama intercepted seven A&M passes and recovered five Aggie fumbles.

The Tide's Jimmy Nelson returned a punt seventy-two yards for a touchdown and rolled up more than one-fourth of Alabama's total yardage for the game when he scampered twenty-one yards for another score. All-American end Holt Rast returned an interception for a touchdown that brought the score to 29–7 before A&M scored two late touchdowns.

Life is just strange, isn't it? How else to explain the college-bowl situation, tattoos, curling, tofu, and teenagers?

Babies don't have kneecaps, some people really don't care about the Iron Bowl, about forty thousand Americans are injured each year by toilets, Dr. Phil is a celebrity—strange is all around us!

Try this on for strangeness: The Almighty God of the universe let himself be killed by being nailed to a couple of pieces of wood. But wait, it gets stranger. He climbed up that cross because he loved you.

It may sound strange, but many champions are made champions by setbacks.
—Olympic champion Bob Richards

    Many things in life are strange, including God's allowing himself to be killed on a cross; but it's true, and it's because of his great love for you.

Regrets, Anyone?

Read 2 Corinthians 7:8–12.

"Godly grief produces a repentance that leads to salvation and brings no regret" (v. 10).

Tommy Lewis once made a sure, open-field tackle for the Crimson Tide—and he deeply regretted it.

Lewis lettered three years for the Tide and scored two touchdowns in the 61–6 blasting of Syracuse in the 1953 Orange Bowl. Lewis's undesired claim to fame, though, came in the 1954 Cotton Bowl, a 28–6 loss to Rice University.

As Clyde Bolton recounted in *The Crimson Tide,* Rice led only 7–6 in the second quarter and was backed up to its five. But Owls running back Dick Moegle swept around right end and broke into the clear, on his way to a ninety-five-yard touchdown run.

Until suddenly Lewis, "bareheaded, charged off the Alabama bench and decked Moegle." Even Lewis couldn't believe he had done it. "I kept telling myself, 'I didn't do it, I didn't do it.' But I knew I had," he said after the game. "I'm just too full of Alabama. He just ran too close."

Lewis went to the Rice dressing room and apologized at halftime. Even Moegle said, "I felt real sorry for him."

The officials awarded Moegle a touchdown on the play. Bolton cited the *Dallas Morning News* report that Lewis, abject and apologizing, walked out of the stadium after the game "with his arm around Moegle."

No one gets through life without a few regrets. You've surely got some. Maybe it's not giving that relationship one last try. Or the time you left the game early and Alabama won it with a last-minute touchdown while you were in the parking lot wondering what all the cheering was about. Maybe you realized recently that you've been working so hard to support your children that they're growing up without you.

Truth is, you probably aren't finished saddling yourself with regrets. But take heart, because there's one action you'll never regret: making God a part of your life.

> *I have no regrets because I know I did my best—*
> *all I could do.*
> —Figure skater Midori Ito

> **Regrets are part of living, but you'll never regret living for God.**

If God Were a Person

Read John 1:1–18.

"The Word was God. . . . And the Word became flesh and lived among us, and we have seen his glory, the glory as of a father's only son" (vv. 1, 14).

If God were a person, would he look like Bear Bryant?

Some folks might think so. After all, as Chris Warner noted in *SEC Sports Quotes,* Alabama senator Jeremiah Denton once said, "We believe that on the eighth day, the Lord created the Crimson Tide." If the Lord has such a personal interest in the Tide, why wouldn't the greatest coach in the history of college football have a direct link to the divine?

Richard Scott said in *Legends of Alabama Football* that the Bear was "widely regarded as a god in college football circles and throughout the South. Some even capitalized the G and believed that, yes, he really did walk on water."

It wasn't just that Bryant was a great coach; it was much more than that. He had presence. Alabama's director of athletics Mal Moore played and coached under Bryant, and he agreed that whatever Bryant had, "whatever it was, he had a lot of it. He had something about him that people simply didn't have or don't have."

George Blanda, star quarterback at Kentucky and in the NFL, remembered the first time he saw Bryant, and he was direct about what he felt. When the coach walked into a team meeting, Blanda thought, "This must be what God looks like."

What do you think God looks like? An old man with long white hair and a flowing white robe who sits on a throne? A spirit—no body at all?

As fans do with Bear Bryant, we frequently attribute to persons we admire or love "godly" qualities. Maybe you know someone who commands such respect and awe from you.

While you may not know for sure what God looks like, you can recognize God's attributes, especially love. God has been a living, breathing person. His name is Jesus, and someday we'll see him face to face.

> *There ought to be two Hall of Fames, one for Coach Bryant and one for everybody else.*
> —Ozzie Newsome

▷ **You may have your own image of God, but for thirty-plus years, two millennia ago, he looked like a man named Jesus.**

In Remembrance

Read 1 Corinthians 11:23–26.

"Do this in remembrance of me" (v. 24).

Alabama team doctor Jeff Lubenthal had called him a "heart-and-lung machine," according to sportswriter Mike Fish in "Remembering David Kimani."

But suddenly the heart stopped.

David Kimani was twenty-five years old when he dropped dead in April 2003 in a campus dining hall. His sudden death was unbelievable. Kimani was one of the best-conditioned athletes in the world, a runner who, as a friend told Fish, had "more miles on his feet than a lot of people have on their cars."

Despite his shortened career, Kimani won six NCAA championships. He was a thirteen-time all-American and was twice the SEC Cross Country Athlete of the Year.

But Kimani's athletic ability wasn't what people remembered first in the aftermath of his death. Fish wrote that Kimani's "warm, endearing smile" was legendary around Tuscaloosa, and he was described in terms like "humble, genuine, and gracious." Alabama head track coach Harvey Glance said of Kimani in "University of Alabama Track Athlete David Kimani Dies," "In all my travels, I never heard one bad thing said about David, and that's a true testament to him and his life. He always had a smile."

Lubenthal, a close friend and a former Crimson Tide baseball player, told Fish, Kimani "is the only athlete I ever took care of that I honestly would say to myself, 'I wish I was more like David.'"

How will you be remembered when you die? You will die, you know.

What determines whether your death leaves a gaping hole in the lives of those with whom you shared your life or a pothole that's quickly paved over? What determines whether those nice words someone will say about you are heartfelt truth or pleasant fabrications that everybody knows aren't so? What determines whether the tears that fall will be from heartfelt grief or a sinus infection?

Love does. The love you give away—not the toys you accumulate—decides how you will be remembered.

> *I don't want people to forget Babe Ruth.*
> *I just want them to remember Henry Aaron.*
> —HENRY AARON

> *How you will be remembered after you die is largely determined by how much and how deeply you love others now.*

Homework

Read Luke 2:39–52.

"After three days they found him in the temple, sitting among the teachers, listening to them and asking them questions. And all who heard him were amazed at his understanding and his answers" (vv. 46–47).

The exploits of the women of the Alabama gymnastics program are now the stuff of legend.

Their third-place finish in the NCAA finals in 2006 was the program's twenty-first final-four finish. Since the program began in 1975, Crimson Tide gymnasts have won five SEC crowns, twenty-one regional titles, and four national championships. More than two hundred Alabama gymnasts have been named all-American.

But the young women who have represented Alabama so well as gymnasts also have racked up legendary achievements in another arena: the classroom. Through 2006 Alabama gymnasts had earned ten NCAA Postgraduate Scholarships, the most in the nation, and 107 Scholastic all-American honors.

The 2006 team was typical. The article "Nine UA Gymnasts" said the squad had a 3.4 grade-point average, with Cassie Martin and Brittany Magee posting perfect 4.0 GPAs.

Coach Sarah Patterson, who is a four-time national Coach of the Year and a member of the Alabama Sports Hall of Fame, said in "Alabama's Academic Success," "From the day we begin recruiting an athlete to the day they walk across the stage at graduation, we stress academics as the most important aspect of their experience here at Alabama."

For Patterson and Alabama's gymnasts, homework is not just the study and preparation for gymnastics but study and preparation for classwork and for life.

"Some assembly required." These three words summon chilling images of bicycle parts or computer components spread all around as you try to get from step 2 to step 3. But you'll get through it because you can read the instructions.

It's the same way in life: Some assembly is required, and you need an instruction book. God gave us one; it's probably by your bed or on a living-room table. You can get through life in good shape because you can read God's instructions in the Bible. You can study and prepare; you can do your homework.

It's not the will to win, but the will to prepare to win that makes the difference.
—Bear Bryant

▷ **You have a readily available set of instructions on how to assemble your life: the Bible.**

Crowd Control

Read Matthew 27:15–26.

"When Pilate saw that he could do nothing, but rather that a riot was beginning, he took some water and washed his hands before the crowd" (v. 24).

It would be nice if history told us the Alabama-Tennessee rivalry began as it is today: with splendid, intense, and superb play. Alas, their first game in 1901 was a disappointing 6–6 tie that ended with "two thousand fans on the field fighting," according to Al Browning in *Third Saturday in October*.

It wasn't the players' fault the game was such a dud. The problem was the crowd: They wouldn't stay off the playing field. As the *Birmingham News* reported and Browning cited, "After almost every down the spectators would rush across the sidelines and form a compact ring around the struggling teams, preventing beyond any possibility any further play."

Some citizens took it upon themselves to try to keep the crowd under control so the game could continue, enlisting the help of a squad of policemen. Their efforts were fruitless, as the majority of fans "rushed at will upon the gridiron, forcing officials to call time until the players could secure more room."

Finally, in the second half, a hot dispute arose until "the affair was hopelessly entangled." It didn't make much difference, however, because efforts at crowd control had consumed so much time that descending darkness would have forced an end to the game anyway.

Teenagers seem to catch particular grief about going along with the crowd, but they aren't alone in allowing others to influence their behavior. Adults, too, often behave in ways contrary to what their conscience tells them is right simply because they fear the disapproval of the people they're with at the time.

So they chuckle at a racial joke. Make fun of a coworker nobody likes. Drink too much and stay out too late. Remain silent when God is cursed.

It remains true, though: Just because the crowd does it doesn't make it right. Even Pontius Pilate understood that.

Never compromise what you think is right.
—BEAR BRYANT

▶ **Just because everybody's doing it doesn't make it right.**

Answering the Call

Read 1 Samuel 3:1–18.

"The LORD came and stood there, calling as before, 'Samuel! Samuel!' And Samuel said, 'Speak, for your servant is listening'" (v. 10).

Sometimes circumstances conspire to place a call upon a life that can't be ignored. They did for Bear Bryant.

In *Legends of Alabama Football* Richard Scott recounted that Bryant's first head-coaching job was at Maryland. He quit after one season (6–2–1) in a dispute with the school president over team discipline and landed at Kentucky. His record over eight seasons in Lexington was 60–23–5, including the school's first SEC championship, but basketball (and Adolph Rupp) was king in Kentucky. Bryant left for Texas A&M in 1954.

His success in College Station was immediate, 7–2–1 in 1955 and 9–0–1 in 1956, with a win over Texas and the Southwest Conference title. The Aggies were 8–0 in 1957 when the call came. Alabama needed him.

Clyde Bolton wrote in *The Crimson Tide* that the decision to leave College Station was not an easy one for Bryant. "This is the most difficult thing I ever had to do," Bryant told reporters when the news of his hiring broke. "You don't stay at Texas A&M as long as we did without learning to love it, the traditions, the boys, everything." Then why did he leave? "The reason, the only reason, I'm going back is because my school called me."

Or as it's usually expressed, "Mama called."

Cleveland? Zambia? A minister? A missionary?

Talk about scary.

You hear stories about God "calling" someone, telling a person what to do with his or her life. That means one thing, right? Moving the family halfway around the world to a place where the folks have never heard of air-conditioning, baseball, or paved roads—and being a minister of some sort.

Not for you, no thank you. And who can blame you?

But most often God calls folks to serve him where they are. In fact, God put you where you are right now. Are you serving him there?

It's how you show up at the showdown that counts.
—TEXAS A&M COACH HOMER NORTON

≫ **Serving God doesn't necessarily mean entering full-time ministry and going to a foreign land; God calls you to serve him right where you are.**

From Tears to Triumph

Read Matthew 27:45–50, 55–61.

"Many women were also there, looking on from a distance; they had followed Jesus from Galilee and had provided for him" (v. 55).

She was thirty-one with plans to marry soon. She was the first assistant Rick Moody hired when he became the head coach of the Alabama women's basketball team before the 1990 season.

And suddenly Dottie Kelso was dead.

Wayne Atcheson related in *Faith of the Crimson Tide* that Moody was fishing on September 15, 1993, when he returned to his truck and found a note instructing him to call the athletic department. That's how he learned Kelso had lapsed into a coma while undergoing tests for her frequent migraines.

Moody rushed to the hospital. "I felt if I could just get there, she would respond to me and would make it," he said. He did, but she didn't, dying from a cyst that had burst in her brain.

Moody said delivering Kelso's eulogy "was the most difficult thing I've ever had to deal with," but his tears were tempered by triumph. A few days before she died, Kelso spoke at a meeting of the Alabama Fellowship of Christian Athletes. She had been scheduled to speak on what would have been the day after she was buried, but she agreed to speak earlier after a cancellation. Thus one of Dottie Kelso's last acts was to witness for her Christian faith.

Though death is an inevitable part of the human experience, nothing can fill us with a more overwhelming sense of loss than the death of a colleague or a loved one.

You're a problem solver; you believe things can be fixed. And then you run head-on into death. In its inexorable reality, death reduces you to standing helplessly and weeping as something precious and beautiful exits your life.

Your tears can also signify a time of triumph, though, if your loved one trusted in Jesus. Your loss is the deceased's gain. Amid death you also find life; amid sorrow you find hope.

The triumph cannot be had without the struggle.
—Wilma Rudolph

➣ **Faith in Jesus Christ transforms death from the ultimate defeat to the ultimate victory.**

A Hollywood Ending

Read Luke 24:1–12.

"Why do you look for the living among the dead? He is not here, but has risen" (v. 5).

For one of Alabama's greatest football players ever, life literally had a Hollywood ending.

Johnny Mack Brown ran his way into college football history when he scored two touchdowns in Alabama's 20–19 win over Washington in the 1926 Rose Bowl, the game that earned southern football its first national respect. With his rugged good looks, Brown was a favorite of the California photographers covering the game. According to Richard Scott's *Legends of Alabama Football,* one sportswriter quipped that Brown would have "enough experience posing for the cameramen to enter the movies" after the Rose Bowl was over.

It turned out that's exactly what Brown did.

He took a screen test in 1927, when he returned to the Rose Bowl as a spectator, and did well enough to land a contract with MGM. After a few small roles, Brown settled into the image that was to make him famous: that of the "cowboy hero willing and able to fight injustice." He made more than 160 movies, including films with John Wayne and Greta Garbo.

Johnny Mack Brown may well be the only person to be in both the College Football Hall of Fame and the Rose Bowl Hall of Fame and also have a star on the Hollywood Boulevard Walk of Fame.

Don't you love movies with a good ending? Boy gets girl; the working man keeps the family land thanks to a last-minute windfall; or Johnny Mack Brown rides up in the nick of time to save the farmer and his beautiful daughter from the evil cattle baron.

We like happy endings because we want to believe that everything in life can be all right. The greatest Hollywood ending of them all, though, was written on a Sunday morning centuries ago when Jesus left a tomb and death behind. With faith in Jesus, your life can have that same ending.

> *This field, this game, is a part of our past, Ray. It reminds us of all that once was good, and that could be again.*
> —JAMES EARL JONES IN *FIELD OF DREAMS*

> **Hollywood doesn't have a patent on happy endings; Jesus has been producing them for almost two millennia.**

Baggage Check

Read Luke 5:17–26.

"Who can forgive sins but God alone?" (v. 21).

When you're about to make history, pack an overnight bag."

As Eli Gold wrote in *Crimson Nation,* that's the lesson John Mitchell learned after a visit to Bear Bryant's office in 1973. But then again, John Mitchell rewrote history with practically every move he made in Tuscaloosa.

Mitchell was Alabama's first African-American football player. As a senior in 1972 he led the SEC champions in sacks and assisted tackles. He became the first African-American in Tide history to be named all-American. He made more history by being the first black player named cocaptain.

After finishing at Alabama, Mitchell entered graduate school and phoned Bryant one day with an offer to do anything he could to help. Bryant told him to drive up from Mobile and then stunned him by offering him a full-time coaching job.

"I didn't know what to say," Mitchell told the *Pittsburgh Post-Gazette* in 2004. "But it was Coach Bryant. I said, 'Yes.' He said, 'Go to work.'"

Mitchell had a problem, though. He told Bryant, "I don't have any clothes." The coach simply looked at him and said, "You'll be all right until Friday. You can go home then and get some."

And so the lesson about history and an overnight bag as John Mitchell became Alabama's first-ever African-American assistant coach.

You arrived and your luggage didn't. Felt just like John Mitchell, didn't you?

The key to successful traveling is not going without baggage but taking along only what you need. This applies to our lives, too, but often we lug along excess baggage: the recriminations we carry from the mistakes we've made, the results of the bad judgment we've shown, the regrets from the love we failed to give.

If only you could dump all that baggage on somebody else with shoulders broad enough to take the whole load and set you free. Somebody . . . like God.

Why buy good luggage? You only use it when you travel.
—YOGI BERRA

> **One of the most heartbreaking mistakes many people make is believing the things they've done are too awful for God to forgive.**

Seeing the Vision

Read Acts 26:1, 9–23.

"After that, . . . I was not disobedient to the heavenly vision" (v. 19).

Every true Alabama fan at one time or another should make a pilgrimage to the Wall of Champions and Bryant-Denny Stadium, which until 1975 was simply Denny Stadium. But how many contemporary Crimson Tide fans know who this Denny guy was?

He was, in fact, the great visionary of Alabama football. William G. Little, the student who introduced football to Alabama's students, had a little of the prophet in him. In *Crimson Nation,* Eli Gold quoted Little as saying, "Football is the game of the future in college life." This was in the nineteenth century, mind you.

But it was Dr. George Hutcheson Denny, president of the University of Alabama from 1912 to 1936, whose vision changed the course of the university's history forever. Denny saw in football something more than a way to keep young men out of trouble and alumni in touch with their school. Gold said Denny "saw football as a means to help Alabama grow in reputation and in stature." He "was the first president to look at the big picture." During Denny's tenure Alabama grew from five hundred students to nearly five thousand, and the football team won five national championships.

His vision set the course toward greatness on which the university remains today.

To speak of visions is often to risk their being lumped with palm readings, Ouija boards, séances, and other mumbo-jumbo. Horoscopes are for mild amusement; a medium is a steak.

You probably do, however, have a vision for your life—a plan for how it should unfold. It's the dream you pursue through your family, your job, your hobbies, your interests. God, too, has a vision for your life, and as the apostle Paul found out, you ignore it at your peril. But if you follow it, you'll find an even more glorious life than you could have envisioned for yourself.

> *If I could see into the future, I wouldn't be sitting here talking to you doorknobs. I'd be out investing in the stock market.*
> —Boston Celtic Kevin McHale

> ⟫ **Your grandest vision for the future will pale beside the vision God has of what the two of you can accomplish together.**

Resting Easy

Read Hebrews 4:1–11.

"A sabbath rest still remains for the people of God; for those who enter God's rest also cease from their labors as God did from his. Let us therefore make every effort to enter that rest" (vv. 9–11).

Bear Bryant's hold over his players and coaches was so complete that he was in control even when he was asleep.

Bryant called John Hannah "the best offensive lineman I ever coached," according to Richard Scott's *Legends of Alabama Football*. Hannah was an all-American guard at Bama in 1971–72 and is a member of both the pro and the college football halls of fame. While he was in the NFL, *Sports Illustrated* put Hannah on its cover with the headline, "The Best Offensive Lineman of All Time."

Hannah told Scott that the players and coaches "were scared to death" of the Bear. He said you could always spot "an assistant coach at Alabama because he had one eye on the field and one on the tower." To back up his claim, Hannah recalled one day at practice when Bryant fell asleep up in the legendary tower. He said the players "kept on practicing and practicing and finally the [bull]horn fell off his leg and made a sound and he woke up." Bryant then bellowed, "Take it in," through the bullhorn.

As the players headed toward the field house, running back Johnny Musso looked over at Hannah and said, "I'm glad he wasn't dead. We'd have never gotten off the field."

The couch calls you for a catnap. The recliner acts like a black hole, sucking you into a void. At your desk, at church, in class, even while driving—you can doze off anywhere.

Like many people, you don't get enough rest. There aren't enough hours in the day to do everything, so how can you sacrifice eight of them to sleep?

But rest isn't a waste of time; even God took a break when he finished his creation. And one of his enduring promises to us is of rest: not laziness, but a soul at peace despite the surrounding frenzy.

> *Happiness is being able to lay your head on the pillow at night and sleep.*
> —HERSCHEL WALKER

▶ **God offers true rest that refreshes the spirit and calms the soul despite the surrounding chaos.**

Home-Field Advantage

Read Joshua 24:14–15.

*"Choose this day whom you will serve . . . ; but as for me
and my household, we will serve the LORD" (v. 15).*

In large part, basketball at Alabama in the early days was
viewed as something the football players did in the off-season
to stay in shape.

A 1938 newspaper article quoted by Clyde Bolton in *The
Basketball Tide* illustrates the casual approach to the game at
the Capstone: "Alabama will go into its initial contest greatly
handicapped by lack of practice because most of the basket-
ballers accompanied the football squad to California."

The student body was clearly into the games, however,
doing its best to give the Crimson Tide a home-field advantage—though in 1927 their actions hadn't been regarded as
commendable by all hands. An editorial in the *Crimson White*
chastised students for their unruly behavior at a game against
Birmingham Southern. "Not content with 'booing' and 'hiss-
ing' the referee," the incensed editor wrote, the rowdies "have
done everything in their power to distract the attention of the
visiting players while they are attempting to shoot fouls."

Surely spinning in his grave at the conduct of students at today's games, the editor concluded his high-minded sentiments with the pronouncement that the "'razzing' of visiting players is a most despicable practice."

Yeah, but it sure is fun, and it sure does help the home team.

Whether it's a condo, an apartment, a two-story mansion, a sprawling ranch house, or a country place with a wraparound porch, you know it as home. For you it's much more than a place to hang out for a while before you crash. You enter to find love, security, and joy. It's the place where your heart feels warmest, your laughter comes easiest, and your life is its richest. It is the center of and the reason for everything you do and everything you are.

How can a home be such a place? By making God part of the family.

Having a home away from the media glare is important to world-class athletes.

—MARY LOU RETTON

▷ **A home is full when all the family members are present—including God.**

Throwing In the Towel

Read Numbers 13:25–14:4.

"The men who had gone up with him said, 'We are not able to go up against this people, for they are stronger than we'" *(v. 31).*

Tommy Wilcox quit.

The same Tommy Wilcox who was a two-time all-American safety and a member of the Alabama Team of the Century. That one.

In 1978, his freshman year, he was redshirted. In the summer of 1979 he decided he wasn't going back to Tuscaloosa. "I figured I'd just hang around close to home and go to one of those other schools," he told Richard Scott in *Legends of Alabama Football*.

But Bear Bryant had other ideas. He called Wilcox, met him at the airport, and walked him to a nearby motel, and then sat down with him face to face. Wilcox recalled that the room had a little table with two chairs, and Bryant arranged the chairs "so that when I sat down and he sat down, his legs were on the outside of mine and my legs were stuck close together." The intimidation had begun.

Bryant's first words set the stage: "Boy, what's your problem?" The great motivator then listened to Wilcox's story and eventually convinced him that if he came back to the Alabama campus, he could not only play but become an all-American. Bryant gave Wilcox three days to think about it. "Needless to say," Wilcox said, "I was back at school in three days."

He didn't quit again.

Remember that time you quit a high-school sports team? Bailed out of a relationship when the word *commitment* came up? Walked away from that job? Parts of your life will remain unfinished because you can never go back and complete them. All you can do now is ponder the possibilities of "What if?"

The next time you're tempted to give up on something or someone, remember the people of Israel, who quit when their goal of a land of their own was within reach. They forgot one fact of life you never should: With God, anything's possible.

The first time you quit, it's hard. The second time, it gets easier. The third time, you don't even have to think about it.
—BEAR BRYANT

> **Whatever else you give up on in your life, don't give up on God. He will never ever give up on you.**

Upon My Word!

Read James 3:1–12.

"No one can tame the tongue—a restless evil, full of deadly poison. With it we bless the Lord *and Father, and with it we curse those who are made in the likeness of God" (vv. 8–9).*

Legendary Alabama football coach Frank Thomas was a master of the dressing-room pep talk.

In Al Browning's *Third Saturday in October,* the great Harry Gilmer recalled the talk Thomas gave his players before the 1946 Rose Bowl against Southern Cal. The words were simple and repetitious, but they had their effect.

Gilmer said Thomas started off whispering three words: "Block and tackle." He kept repeating them, gradually letting his voice grow louder. Finally Thomas turned to tackle Vaughn Mancha, "started screaming 'block and tackle,' and started pounding Mancha on his helmet. Then he screamed, 'Let's go get them!' "

The fired-up Crimson Tide players all dashed toward the dressing-room doors—and wound up in one confused wad with nowhere to go. As they surged forward, the excited players discovered the doors had to be pulled open, not pushed. So they had to back up and start over. Gilmer said, "I literally stepped on top of four or five teammates trying to get to the field."

But Thomas's words could truly motivate his players. Gilmer said, "Just when I thought I'd heard it all from him, he'd come up with some other way to send chills down my spine."

The Tide won that Rose Bowl 34–14 to finish undefeated.

Don't you hate it when a commercial comes on TV louder than the program you were watching? It's just a tactic to get your attention so you can hear what they've got to say, but it's annoying still.

Everybody's got something to say. What about you? Your words are perhaps the most powerful force you possess for good or for bad. The words you speak today can belittle, wound, humiliate, and destroy. Or they can inspire, heal, protect, and build up.

What you say is important; others are always listening and being affected. Choose every word carefully.

Words can be like baseball bats when used maliciously.
—AUTHOR SIDNEY MADWED

> **Your words are the most powerful force you have—for good or for bad.**

The Sure Foundation

Read Luke 6:46–49.

"I will show you what someone is like who comes to me, hears my words, and acts on them. That one is like a man building a house, who dug deeply and laid the foundation on rock" (vv. 47–48).

They were dismal numbers: 4–20; 8–18; 10–16.

Those were the records of Coach C. M. Newton's first three men's basketball teams at Alabama. So how is it that, as Clyde Bolton wrote in *The Basketball Tide,* Newton had only four pictures of Alabama players on the walls of his office: the seniors on that 4–20 team of 1969? "They contributed as much as anybody to building our program," Newton explained.

In those early seasons Newton built a foundation for success.

It wasn't easy. In 1969 the Tide manager accidentally wandered into a Tennessee practice the day before a game in Knoxville. To his dismay and embarrassment, he saw that the Volunteers weren't even preparing for Alabama but for LSU, their opponent after the Tide.

Even Newton began to wonder as the losses mounted: "I

knew what we needed to do and what we wanted to do, and I thought I knew how to do it. But I got to where I had doubts."

The foundation was laid, though. In 1972 Alabama went 18–8, and a new era had begun. Over the following nine seasons of Newton's tenure, the Crimson Tide won three SEC championships and landed in the NCAA Tournament twice and the National Invitation Tournament four times. The record was 189–69, the best run in Alabama basketball history.

Your life is a continuing project, a work in progress. Like any complex construction job, though, if your life is to be stable, it must have a solid foundation. Otherwise, like a basketball team that can't recover from a heartbreaking loss, your life heads downhill at the first trouble that comes your way.

R. Alan Culpepper commented in *The New Interpreter's Bible*, "We do not choose whether we will face severe storms in life; we only get to choose the foundation on which we will stand."

The one sure foundation is Jesus Christ.

First master the fundamentals.
—LARRY BIRD

> *In building your life, you must start with a solid foundation, or the first trouble that shows up will knock you down.*

DAY 86

Cuss Words

Read Psalm 19:14.

"Let the words of my mouth and the meditation of my heart be acceptable to you, O Lord."

Vomit buckets.

Their presence announced a new day for Alabama football in 1958.

The Crimson Tide needed some changes. From 1955 to 1957 the record was 4–24–2, unbelievable at a school with Alabama's rich gridiron tradition.

And then Bear Bryant showed up. Richard Scott said in *Legends of Alabama Football* that what greeted the Tide football players in 1958 was a "level of stringent demands" beyond even the legendary torment of Junction, Texas, during Bryant's first year at Texas A&M. The vomit buckets in the gymnasium on the top floor of Friedman Hall served notice of what lay in store.

But Bryant wasn't cruel just to uphold his reputation. He knew that to win, Alabama needed a change in attitude. Clyde Bolton said in *The Crimson Tide* that Bryant realized two things had to take place: "getting the material and teaching your kids to forget a losing complex."

Torturous training and stringent rules were part of that teaching, that changing of the attitude. Being cussed out was not part of the training, however. One of the new rules Bryant instituted was a ban on cursing that did not exclude him. Profanity was punishable by a twenty-five-cent fine for the players, one dollar for the coaches, and ten bucks for the head coach himself.

Honestly answer these indelicate questions: With what name did you christen that slow driver you couldn't pass? What unflattering words did you have for that stubborn golf ball that wouldn't stay in the fairway?

We live in a coarsened culture when words no one would utter in polite society a few decades ago now spew from our music and our televisions—and our own mouths.

Some argue that profane language is really harmless expression. Our words, however, reveal what's in our hearts, and what God seeks there is love and gentleness, not vileness.

American professional athletes are bilingual; they speak English and profanity.
—NHL LEGEND GORDIE HOWE

➤ **Our words—including profane ones—expose what is in our hearts.**

Trustworthy

Read Psalm 25.

"To you, O Lord, I lift up my soul. O my God, in you I trust" (vv. 1–2).

Buy a ring or eat?

Chad Goss decided to trust God.

Goss came to the Capstone in 1993 as a walk-on football player. Leah Monteith came at the same time as a scholarshipped basketball player.

As Wayne Atcheson told their story in *Faith of the Crimson Tide,* they met as freshmen through their association with the Fellowship of Christian Athletes. They fell in love, and Goss spent the summer before his junior year trying to earn enough money to buy Monteith an engagement ring.

But Goss faced a difficult choice when the summer ended. He still had no scholarship. "It was like, do I want to buy a ring or do I want to eat this semester," he said. In his quandary, he turned to God. "I just had to trust God. I told God, I believe that what you want for my life is to marry Leah."

So he took a leap of faith, proposing to Monteith when she

came back in the fall at lunch in between his two-a-day practices. He gave her the ring.

The next day at practice, Goss "made a miraculous catch. It was just God." The day after that, Coach Gene Stallings called five players into his office and gave them scholarships. One of them was Chad Goss.

Ever heard the claim that a juice from some fruit you never heard of from some foreign country can heal every ailment you have? If some ad offers you a weekend at the beach for practically nothing, you know there's a time-share spiel coming, right? And don't even mention that exercise machine that will "melt" the pounds off.

This modern age has eroded much of a part of us we'd all like to have back: our trusting nature. Which is why many of us don't trust God: We're looking for the catch. The good news is, there isn't one.

> *Good teams become great ones when the members trust*
> *each other enough to surrender the "me" for the "we."*
> —NBA COACH PHIL JACKSON

➤ **We look for the scam before surrendering our trust;**
but with God, there's no spin. We can trust him with-
out hesitation.

Please!

Read Matthew 7:7–11.

"Ask, and it will be given you; search, and you will find; knock, and the door will be opened for you" (v. 7).

Senior linebacker Barry Krauss made the tackle on what Richard Scott in *Legends of Alabama Football* said was "perhaps the most famous play in Alabama football history." But Krauss wouldn't have even been on the team if he hadn't begged Bear Bryant for a second chance.

The famous play was the fourth-quarter, fourth-down tackle at the goal line in the 1979 Sugar Bowl against Penn State that preserved a 14–7 Alabama win and the national championship.

As a sophomore Krauss had missed curfew and went by Bryant's office to beg for forgiveness. He told Scott about the meeting.

He started by apologizing. "Coach Bryant just had his head down, and he wouldn't even look at me." Krauss apologized again. The "next thing I know I'm crying" and apologizing "and looking at him with one eye open, but he still wasn't looking at me."

Krauss then did what all great athletes do when the pressure is on: He elevated his game—only this time it was to crying and pleading. Finally Bryant looked up "and mumbled something about straightening up. I promised I would and took off as fast as I could."

Did it make a difference? Krauss's roommate, who had also violated curfew, didn't go to see Bryant. He lost his scholarship and was kicked out of the dorm.

Whether it's for the one you love to marry you, for a raise, for justice in traffic court—you'll ask for what you want, but you won't beg. Western society still stigmatizes begging. You may hand some money to the person holding a pleading sign along the road, but you probably also wonder why that beggar doesn't get a job.

Like Barry Krauss's meeting with Bear Bryant, begging is born of desperation, when it's all you have left. But God doesn't want you coming to him just as a last resort, so God asks only that you ask—not beg.

Never be too proud to get down on your knees and pray.
—BEAR BRYANT

> *God doesn't require that you beg, only that you ask.*

The Big Time

Read Matthew 2:19–23.

"He made his home in a town called Nazareth" (v. 23).

Paul William "Bear" Bryant called himself "a simple plow hand from Arkansas," wrote *Legends of Alabama Football* author Richard Scott. And he was. Yet he made an improbable run from the backwoods to the big time.

Bryant wasn't born in a decent town but in a place called Moro Bottom in southern Arkansas. Scott described Moro Bottom as "a three-square-mile plot of land where seven families lived near Moro Creek."

As a boy Bryant chopped cotton for fifty cents a day and peddled vegetables from a wagon. When he was fourteen years old, he participated in the most legendary bear story this side of Davy Crockett. He wrestled a carnival bear for a dollar. Bryant didn't get the money, but he did get a lifelong nickname.

Football was Bryant's ticket out of poverty. Clyde Bolton wrote in *The Crimson Tide* that when Bryant made the high-school football team, he "had cleats put on the only pair of shoes he owned and wore them everywhere, to practice, to school, to church."

The "simple plow hand" went on to hit it big: 323 wins to break Amos Alonzo Stagg's record; six national championships and thirteen SEC titles at Alabama; National Coach of the Year three times and SEC Coach of the Year ten times.

The stage on which you play out your life may be far removed from the bright lights of Broadway, the glitz of Hollywood, or the halls of power in Washington, D.C. You may, in fact, have grown up in a virtually unknown village in a backwater county. You may even now be living your adult life in an out-of-the-way region of a largely ignored state.

If so, then you have much in common with the Bear—and with Jesus, who also came from a small, disrespected town.

Where you live doesn't matter. How you live does.

I live so far out in the country that I have to walk toward town to go hunting.
—Former major leaguer Rocky Bridges

≫ **Where you live may be the result of circumstances; how you live is a choice you make.**

Amazing!

Read Matthew 28:1–10.

"I know that you are looking for Jesus who was crucified. He is not here; for he has been raised, as he said"
(vv. 5–6).

The Crimson Tide was a tick of the clock away from losing the first game the school ever played in a national basketball tournament. And then Glenn Garrett did something amazing.

Under Coach C. M. Newton, the 1973 team was 22–8, a school record for victories. They finished second in the SEC to Kentucky, which in those days earned the Tide a spot in the National Invitation Tournament in New York. The first-round opponent was Manhattan.

Four of Alabama's starters made all-SEC: Wendell Hudson and Charles Cleveland were first-team; Leon Douglas and Ray Odums were second-team. And then there was Glenn "Goober" Garrett, the fifth starter. Clyde Bolton said in *The Basketball Tide* that Garrett "played basketball on hustle and dogged defense."

With eleven seconds to play, Manhattan led 86–85. Bama had the ball out of bounds, but Paul Ellis had to bring it the length of the floor, and Manhattan pressured him all the way. Finally he gave it to Garrett, who let it fly with a desperate jump shot from twenty-two feet as the buzzer sounded. He hit nothing but net, and Alabama won 87–86.

The shot wasn't just the longest one Garrett ever made in a game. He told Bolton it was the longest shot he ever took in a game.

The word *amazing* has to do with the limits of what you believe to be plausible or usual. The Grand Canyon, the birth of your children, those last-second Alabama wins—they're amazing!

The really amazing aspect of your life, though, is not the sights you've seen, the places you've been, the people you've met and loved, or the things you've experienced. All that—everything—pales beside God's walking around on earth, letting people take his life . . . and then not staying dead.

Most amazing of all is why God did such a thing: because he loves you.

A hole in one is amazing when you think of the different universes this white mass of molecules has to pass through on its way to the hole.
—Pro golfer Mac O'Grady

> **God let humans kill him—and then refused to stay dead. That's amazing, but the best part is that he did it for you.**

BIBLIOGRAPHY

Angel Fire. "Description of Uniforms by Year." http://www.angelfire.com/al/bamacrimsontide/uniforms.html.

Atcheson, Wayne. *Faith of the Crimson Tide*. Grand Island, NE: Cross Training Publishing, 2000.

Bolton, Clyde. *The Basketball Tide: A Story of Alabama Basketball*. Huntsville, AL: The Strode Publishers, Inc., 1977.

———. *The Crimson Tide: A Story of Alabama Football*. Huntsville, AL: The Strode Publishers, 1972.

Browning, Al. *Third Saturday in October: The Game-by-Game Story of the South's Most Intense Football Rivalry*, 2nd ed. Nashville: Cumberland House, 2001.

Culpepper, R. Alan. "The Gospel of Luke: Introduction, Commentary, and Reflections." *The New Interpreter's Bible,* Vol. IX. Nashville: Abingdon Press, 1995.

Fish, Mike. "Remembering David Kimani." CNN/*Sports Illustrated*. http://sportsillustrated.cnn.com/inside_game/mike_fish/nws/2003/05/02/straight_shooting.

Gold, Eli. *Crimson Nation*. Nashville: Rutledge Hill Press, 2005.

Hughes, Buddy. "Williams Living the American Dream." *Crimson White,* March 2, 2005. http://www.cw.ua.edu/vnews/display.v/ART/2005/03/02/42255dfa69802?in_archive=1.

Lee, Richard D. "Bama Hires Smith." *Crimson White*, April 14, 2005. http://www.cw.ua.edu/vews/display.v/ART/2005/04/14/425e1191e1056?in_archive=1.

———. "Great Scott." *Crimson White*, April 15, 2005. http://www.cw.ua.edu/vnews/display.v/ART/2005/04/15/425f55863e451?in_archive=1.

Lewter, Micah. "Tide Women Score 19 Unanswered Points in Stunning Comeback." *Crimson White*, December 11, 2001. http://www.cw.ua.edu/vnews/display.v/ART/2001/12/11/3c15779478108?in_archive=1.

Patterson, Jessie. "Palmer Retires After 17 Years at Capstone." *Crimson White*, April 27, 2005. http://www.cw.ua.edu/vnews/display.v/ART/2005/04/27/426f4123d72ao?in_archive=1.

———. "Striking a Balance." *Crimson White*, September 29, 2005. http://www.cw.ua.edu/vnews/display.v/ART/2005/09/29/433b7b3d79eea?in_archive=1.

———. "VanBrakle Helps Team to 11–0 Start." *Crimson White*, February 18, 2005. http://www.cw.ua.edu/vnews/display.v/ART/2005/02/18/421593d41ff23?in_archive=1.

Pillion, Dennis. "Still Perfect: Little-Known UA Racquetball Team Repeats National Title." *Crimson White*, April 7, 2005. http://www.cw.ua.edu/vnews/display.v/ART/2005/04/07/4254cfeb2395b?in_archive=1.

Scalici, Matt. "Humphrey Taking Alabama by Storm." *Crimson White,* February 11, 2005. http://www.cw/ua.edu/vnews/display.v/ART/2005/02/11/420c75aea9317?in_archive=1.

———. "Tide's Bayer Has West Coast Flair." *Crimson White,* March 4, 2005. http://www.cw.ua.edu/vnews/display.v/ART/2005/03/04/422813aa59d3d?in_archive=1.

Scott, Richard. *Legends of Alabama Football.* Champaign, IL: Sports Publishing L.L.C., 2004.

Tide Sports. "Nine UA Gymnasts Named Scholastic All-Americans." *Tuscaloosa News.* http://www.tidesports.com/apps/pbcs.dll/article?AID=/20060707/NEWS.

University of Alabama. "Alabama Gymnastics: A Tradition of Excellence—a Legacy of Champions." http://www.rolltide.com/fls/8000/files/gymnastics/2006/mediaguide/06gymmg.

———. "Alabama Legend: Roberta Alison." http:www.rolltide.com/fls/8000/files/wtennis/2004-05/mediaguide.pdf.

———. "Alabama's Academic Success." http://www.rolltide.com/fls/8000/files/gymnastics/2006/mediaguide/06gymmg.

———. "Bryant-Denny Stadium: The History." http://www.rolltide.com/ViewArticle.dbml?&DB_OEM_ID=8000&ATCLID=239832.

———. "Cheerleaders: General Information." http://www. rolltide.com/ViewArticle.dbml?DB_OEM_ ID=8000&ATCLID=240177.

———. "The Elephant Story." http://www.rolltide.com/View-Article.dbml?DB_OEM_ID=8000&ATCLID=239531.

———. "Million Dollar Band: History and Facts." http://www. rolltide.com/ViewArticle.dbml?DB_OEM_ ID=8000&ATCLID=239532.

———. "Safiya Ingram: 2000 NCAA Sportsperson of the Year." http://www.rolltide.com/fls/8000/files/ wtrack/2003-04/mediaguide-40–72.

———. "UA Wins National Intercollegiate Racquetball Championship." http://uanews.ua.edu/anews2004/apr04/rac-quetball042004.htm.

———. "University of Alabama Track Athlete David Kimani Dies." http://www.rolltide.com/ViewArticle.dmbl?DB_ OEM_ID=8000&ATCLID=229974.

Ward, Sela. "Smack Dab in the Middle of It All." Sela Ward Fan Club. http://www.selawardtv.com/bama.html.

Warner, Chris. *SEC Sports Quotes*. Baton Rouge: CEW Enterprises, 2002.

Woodbery, Evan. "Bama Fans Drenched But Cheerful. *Crimson White,* November 30, 2001. http://www.cw.ua.edu/vnews/ display.v/ART/2001/11/30/3c070fc14bdof?in_archive=1.

Now that you've studied the playbook, these ninety winning replays can help you stay on top of your game.

1. God has a vision for your life beyond your imagining, but you have to depend on him, not on yourself.

2. When you go isn't up to you; where you go is.

3. The example of the faithful who persevered despite trepidation and suffering calls you to be true to God no matter what besets you.

4. Faith that does not reveal itself in action is dead.

5. Life demands more than mere physical toughness; you must be spiritually tough, too.

6. Yes, the church needs its professional clergy, but it also needs those who serve as volunteers because they love God; the church needs you.

7. That you make mistakes doesn't mean God will give up on you. He's a God of second chances.

8. Mamas often sacrifice for their children, but God, too, will take drastic measures for his children, including dying for them.

9. When life hits you with pain, turn to God for comfort, consolation, and hope.

10. You have your own peculiar set of fears, but never let them paralyze you; remember that God is greater than anything you fear.

11. The greatest prize of all doesn't require competition to claim it; God has it ready to hand to you.

12. God's heroes are the people who remain steady in their faith while serving others.

13. Fatherhood is a tough job, but a model for the father-child relationship is found in that between Jesus the Son and God the Father.

14. Where Jesus is concerned, clothes don't make the person; faith does.

15. God gives you freedom of choice: life or death. Which will you choose?

16. Life's moments of glory are fleeting; true, eternal glory is the purview of almighty God.

17. Hospitality is an outward sign of the inward loving and generous nature of the host.

18. Material wealth and possessions can clutter a life, but they can never fill it.

19. You may not get the respect you deserve, but dare to succeed anyway.

20. Every dawn is not just a new day; it is a precious chance to begin anew.

21. With Jesus, life is one big party, a celebration of victory and joy.

22. God has a job for you: spreading his love around. Get to work!

23. Unbridled joy can send you jumping all over the place, and Jesus said such exultation should not be something rare but a way of life.

24. The justice you receive from God will depend on the justice you give to others.

25. In life, victory is truly a matter of how you finish and whether you finish with Jesus at your side.

26. The most lopsided victory in all of history is a sure thing: God's ultimate triumph over evil.

27. Because of Jesus, rather than stinking to high heaven, death is the way to high heaven.

28. Making up with others frees you from your past, turning you loose to get on with your richer, fuller future.

29. In our ever-changing and bewildering world, Jesus is the same forever; his love for you will never change.

30. Jesus's presence transforms a funeral from a lamenting of death to a celebration of life.

31. God has a job for you, one for which he has given you particular talents, abilities, and passions.

32. Family, for the followers of Jesus, comes not from a shared ancestry but from a shared faith.

33. With God on your side, you will prevail.

34. In the people of your church, you have your own set of cheerleaders to urge you to greater faithfulness.

35. Your attitude determines more than your mood; it shapes the kind of person you are.

36. Making peace instead of fighting takes courage and strength, but it's certainly the less painful—and wiser—option.

37. You may consider some painting a work of art, but the real masterpiece is you.

38. Success in life takes planning and strategy; success in death does, too, and God has the plan for you.

39. Rather than constraining you, commitment lends meaning to your life, releasing you to pursue your life's purpose.

40. Youth is no excuse for not serving God; it just gives you more time.

41. Whether death is your worst enemy or a solicitous chauffeur is a matter of perspective; where do you stand?

42. A decision for Jesus may be spontaneous or considered; what counts is that you make it.

43. Success isn't permanent, and failure isn't fatal—unless you're talking about your relationship with God.

44. When it comes to looking good, it's what's inside that counts.

45. Faithfulness to God requires faith even in—especially in—the hard times.

46. Be sure you don't allow any riches or luxuries to come before God in your life.

47. God's top-ten list is a set of instructions on how you should conduct yourself with other people and with him.

48. Live so that your name evokes positive associations by people you know, the public, and God.

49. Faith is a lifelong journey of growth.

50. You are deeply in debt to God for everything you have, but what he wants as payback is simply your faith.

51. Jesus expects you to do what he has told you to do—but it's because he loves you and wants the best for you.

52. Dreams based on the world's promises are often crushed; those based on God's promises are a sure thing.

53. Frustration is a vexing part of life, but God expects us to handle it gracefully.

54. In life, you learn and then you teach. This includes learning and teaching about Jesus, the most important lesson of all.

55. You may not have a fine opinion of your body, but God thought enough of it to personally create it for you.

56. God chooses to keep much about himself shrouded in mystery, but one day you will see and understand.

57. Some things hit you so hard, you know you'll never be the same again; God's love is one of those things.

58. You are more than you appear to the world, but you're in good company; many don't know Jesus for who he is either.

59. People, things, and organizations will let you down. Only God deserves our absolute trust and confidence.

60. God's offer of eternal life through Jesus is for a limited time only; it expires at your death. Don't wait till it's too late.

61. Since God is the source of all wisdom, it's only logical that you encounter him with your mind as well as your emotions.

62. It's so good it sounds crazy—but it's not: Through faith in Jesus, you can have eternal life with God.

63. Society's rules dictate who is acceptable and who is not, but love in the name of Jesus knows no such distinctions.

64. We have no secrets before God; good thing he's on our side.

65. Jesus won't barge into your life; he will come in only when you open the door and invite him.

66. A life of faith is lived in certainty and conviction: You just know you know.

67. As far as God is concerned, you can never go wrong doing right.

68. God keeps his promises, just as those who rely on you expect you to keep yours.

69. You call it music; others may call it noise. If it's joyful, send some God's way.

70. Many things in life are strange, including God's allowing himself to be killed on a cross; but it's true, and it's because of his great love for you.

71. Regrets are part of living, but you'll never regret living for God.

72. You may have your own image of God, but for thirty-plus years, two millennia ago, he looked like a man named Jesus.

73. How you will be remembered after you die is largely determined by how much and how deeply you love others now.

74. You have a readily available set of instructions on how to assemble your life: the Bible.

75. Just because everybody's doing it doesn't make it right.

76. Serving God doesn't necessarily mean entering full-time ministry and going to a foreign land; God calls you to serve him right where you are.

77. Faith in Jesus Christ transforms death from the ultimate defeat to the ultimate victory.

78. Hollywood doesn't have a patent on happy endings; Jesus has been producing them for almost two millennia.

79. One of the most heartbreaking mistakes many people make is believing the things they've done are too awful for God to forgive.

80. Your grandest vision for the future will pale beside the vision God has of what the two of you can accomplish together.

81. God offers true rest that refreshes the spirit and calms the soul despite the surrounding chaos.

82. A home is full when all the family members are present—including God.

83. Whatever else you give up on in your life, don't give up on God. He will never ever give up on you.

84. Your words are the most powerful force you have—for good or for bad.

85. In building your life, you must start with a solid foundation, or the first trouble that shows up will knock you down.

86. Our words—including profane ones—expose what is in our hearts.

87. We look for the scam before surrendering our trust; but with God, there's no spin. We can trust him without hesitation.

88. God doesn't require that you beg, only that you ask.

89. Where you live may be the result of circumstances; how you live is a choice you make.

90. God let humans kill him—and then refused to stay dead. That's amazing, but the best part is that he did it for you.

Printed in the United States
by Baker & Taylor Publisher Services